The HATCH Chile Cookbook

The HATCH Chile Cookbook

Hot & Spicy Recipes Featuring the World's Finest Chile Peppers

David G. Jackson and Mark Preston

Border Books
PUBLISHERS

P.O. Box 80780
Albuquerque, New Mexico 87198
(505) 254-0325

Design by Lois Bergthold
Production by Deborah Beldring
Executive Editor: Melissa T. Stock
Copy Editing by Lee Hilles

Printed in the United States of America

ISBN 1-884374-03-4

How to Order:
Quantity discounts are available from Border Books, P.O. Box 80780, Albuquerque, New Mexico
87198; telephone (505) 254-0325. On your letterhead include information concerning the intended
use of the books and the number of books you wish to purchase.

Contents

The HATCH Chile Cookbook

Getting to the Hatch Valley

The Hatch Valley is located on Interstate 25, north from El Paso and south from Albuquerque. It can also be reached by taking New Mexico 6 from Interstate 10 at Deming, and by U.S. 70, east from Roswell. The route through the middle of the farming area is old U.S Highway 85, now New Mexico 187 and 185.

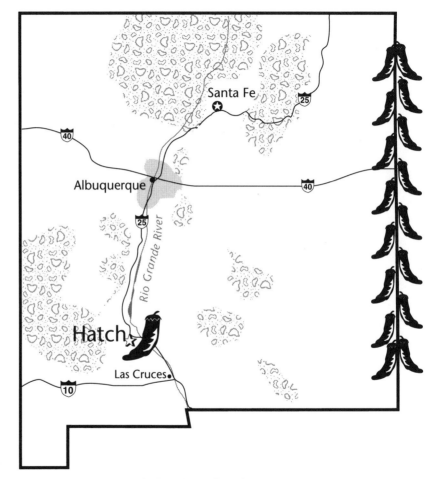

Dear Chile lovers (and lovers to be),

New Mexico style food is recognized as one of the unique regional cuisines in the world. The special flavors of the various chile varieties grown in this state cannot be duplicated—the same recipe made with chile grown elsewhere just doesn't measure up.

HATCH Brand Products, which include everything from enchilada sauce to refried black beans to taco shells, some 40 items in all, are made from the very best ingredients—all grown in the U.S. All of our products are as natural as we can make them. Because our most important goal is quality, our chile is flame roasted, a much slower and more expensive procedure. All of our products are made without lard or MSG. We want only the pure and natural taste of HATCH chile in our products. New products are under development at professional food kitchens which will assure that HATCH Brand continues to provide the best New Mexico style food available. HATCH Brand products are carried by many of the largest grocery chains in the U.S. and are also available by mail order. Ask for them by name!

The recipes in this special cookbook include both traditional and new offerings with something for almost everyone, whether you like it hot, medium or mild. HATCH Brand products add quality ingredients to each dish. Our pledge is to make sure that you get the best New Mexico style food available anywhere.

We hope that you enjoy the fine recipes in this book.

Sincerely,

Steve and Kathleen Dawson
HATCH Brand Products

Chapter One

A Hot History of Hatch

"Welcome to Hatch, New Mexico, Chile Capital of the World," states a rather innocuous sign just off the exit from I-25, a few miles north of Las Cruces. A mighty big claim for a small farming community (population 1,018).

However, due to this very special crop, Hatch is one of the places in the United States which have become synonymous with certain foods. Avery Island, Louisiana, for hot sauce; Gilmore, California, for garlic; Vidalia, Georgia, for onions, to name a few.

In the world of chile, the Hatch Valley of New Mexico has gained the reputation as the best-known source for what is the world's most popular condiment.

Hatch? New Mexico?

How has this small agricultural area, stretching some 40 miles from Elephant Butte Dam south to Radium Hot Springs in the lower Rio Grande Valley of southern New Mexico, gained this fame? There has been no national marketing campaign, no organized tours through the fields and processing plants. Just a small community festival and word of mouth from chile-heads all over the world who know the best when they eat it!

The key ingredient is chile. Although grown in other parts of the country, chile is very special in New Mexico because it is the basic ingredient for New Mexican-style food that has been imitated and, many would say, not successfully reproduced anywhere else.

Although chile products are promoted by the processing industry, it has been mostly by word of mouth that the popularity of chile dishes has spread around the nation and the world. Perhaps it was the many servicemen who have been stationed at the military bases in New Mexico; maybe it was the reporters who have written stories about the delights of fiery food for newspapers, magazines (including "Chile Pepper Magazine," the bible for spicy food lovers) and television programs; or it might have been the hundreds of cookbooks giving New Mexico recipes to gourmet cooks the world over.

Whatever the cause, the use of New Mexico chile is increasing every year. The crop was worth about $130 million in 1993, up from $52 million in 1983. An important component of this growth has been chile from the Hatch Valley, which has set a standard of excellence recognized the world over.

The Hatch Valley is a narrow green strip of fields all within sight of one of America's great rivers, the Rio Grande, which splits the great brown land that is New Mexico. On these fields are grown as many as a dozen varieties of chile that have continued to add to a culinary legend.

Processing and canning factories send the many varieties to the world market in a wide assortment of products, ranging from bricks of frozen green chile, to pickled jalapeños, to salsa, to red powder, to canned green chile. A large percentage of the 60,000 tons of chile produced in New Mexico comes from the Hatch Valley—a significant portion being consumed by the most dedicated chileheads of all, the residents of the Land of Enchantment. To many, New Mexico's addiction to the spicy delights of chile is one of the key ingredients of the state's enchantment.

In the Beginning...

New Mexico was colonized by Spanish settlers in 1598, when Don Juan de Oñate led his band of farmers, soldiers and priests, along with their livestock and farm equipment, into the area across the Rio Grande at *Paseo del Norte*, what is now Juarez, Mexico, and El Paso, Texas. The hardy group followed the river north for about 60 miles through what are now the Mesilla and Hatch valleys, then went east of the mountains to cross a 92-mile stretch of waterless desert they named *Jornada del Muerto*, the Journey of Death. The route was necessary because the land bordering the middle river was too difficult to traverse for the *carretas* or two-wheeled wagons used to carry goods.

Along the way, the settlers passed several Indian villages and cultivated fields—some abandoned. They eventually settled in northern New Mexico on the west side of the Rio Grande, near the San Juan Pueblo along the upper Rio Grande, before founding the city of Santa Fe in 1610. The Spanish were chased from New Mexico in 1680 by the Pueblo Indians. They returned in 1692, rebuilding old settlements and establishing new ones.

In addition to the horses, sheep and cattle that these early Spanish settlers brought, they carried with them seeds for a plant that produced a red pod which was ground into a fiery-hot powder used to flavor native foods—chile. A product of the New World, chile was part of the native diet when the Spanish arrived in the Americas.

The use of chile was quickly embraced by all residents of this wild frontier, and the hot food of New Mexico became a legend of its time—a legend that continues today. It was a favorite of the first mountain men and trappers who came into New Mexico from the north, and was described by early traders on the Santa Fe Trail.

For more than 200 years, few Spanish settlers lived in the lower Rio Grande Valley south of Socorro. The weather was hot, the land was rough and, most important of all, it was the home of the dreaded Apache Indians, nomad warriors who did not want to share their territory with anyone. The road from Mexico City to Santa Fe was know as *El Camino Real*, the Royal Road, and is still in use today (we call it Interstate 25).

Few Spaniards chose to live in the lower Rio Grande Valley until the mid-1800s because the Apache ruled the area. Users of the Camino Real had to travel in heavily armed wagon trains, and even then often suffered grievous losses from Apache attackers. New Mexico was annexed by the United States in 1846 during the war with Mexico, and the job of protecting settlements and pacifying the Indians became the responsibility of the U.S. Army.

Which was easier said than done.

The rich lower Rio Grande Valley had drawn a number of hardy settlers who practiced subsistence irrigation farming, mostly vegetables—including a small amount of native chile. The U.S. Army established a number of small forts along the Rio Grande and in the mountains and valleys to the west to protect the small settlements. It was a hard fight, with the Indians holding their own most of the time. Life on this frontier was rough at best, and the lower Rio Grande Valley continued to be primarily a place people passed through on the way north or south. Still, mining and ranching activities caused these river villages to grow slowly.

Another great change occurred in 1861 when the Civil War came to New Mexico. The Union abandoned southern New Mexico and the Confederacy took over, founding the state of Arizona in the process. In February 1862, a Confederate army marched north from El Paso with the goal of capturing the Colorado gold fields and drawing Union forces from the battlefields in the east. Two battles were fought in New Mexico. The first battle, at Valverde just north of the Hatch Valley, saw the defeat of Union forces, who retreated into nearby Ft. Craig on the west side of the river. The Confederates marched north, taking Albuquerque and Santa Fe, before being defeated by Union volunteers from Colorado at the Battle of Glorietta, north of Santa Fe. The rebel army retreated south into Texas, never to return.

The Union did commit more troops to the frontier, and within 25 years had beaten the Indians and placed them on reservations. The campaign was brutal. Eighteen Congressional Medals of Honor were awarded to troopers for combat against the Indians in New Mexico, many of the battles fought within sight of the Hatch Valley. The last report of a settler killed in the valley by the Indians was in 1884.

The subjugation of the Indians, coupled with the coming of the railroad in the mid-1880s and the discovery of gold, silver and copper in the mountains to the west, encouraged farming in the valley. The town of Hatch and the entire valley were named for General Edward Hatch, a Civil War hero and the military commander credited with ending the career of the famous Apache chief Victorio.

Hatch was established in the early 1880s as a flag station on the Santa Fe Railroad branch between Rincon and Deming. The other valley villages, Arrey, Derry, Garfield, Salem, Rincon, Placitas, Leasburg, and Radium Springs were founded and grew into communities during this period. The old railroad town of Rincon and the ruins of Ft. Selden are reminders of the early days in the valley. The first paved road was built through the area in 1934.

Down Home in Hatch...

Today, the Hatch Valley is a broad area of neatly tilled fields watered by an extensive irrigation system, small communities with sturdy homes, and processing plants of various sizes and kinds. It is a quiet place where the cycle of farming sets the pace of life. The village of Hatch is a dusty community with schools, churches and small businesses that cater to the farmers and to the many tourists that visit the area, particularly during the chile harvest season. The tiny restaurants provide some of the best New Mexico-style chile meals in the state, and local merchants can provide anything from a truckload of fresh chile to decorative ristras and wreaths in seemingly endless designs.

GROWING THE GOOD STUFF...

Cultivating chile is not an easy task. Like all other crops, it has the common requirements of good soil, a dependable water supply, sunshine, seed and people. In terms of cultivation, chile is a lot more particular in its requirements than many other agricultural products.

ABOUT THE LAND

With its headwaters in the high Rocky Mountains of Colorado and New Mexico, the Rio Grande has drained an immense area of both states for millions of years. It is a river which carries large amounts of sediment from all of its tributaries and, as it changed course over the years, has deposited silt in broad flood plains in the valleys in New Mexico and Texas as it flows toward the Gulf of Mexico. The rich soil in these valleys is ideal for the cultivation of a variety of crops, but especially for chile. The irrigated fields go right to the edge of the surrounding desert hills. In season it looks like an undulating pool table as the breeze blows through the ripening chile.

THE WATER

Until 1916, water was a problem in the Hatch Valley.
With an annual rainfall of nine inches, much of which comes in late summer thunderstorms, there was either too little or too much, depending on how much rain fell in the watershed upstream. Diversion dams built to supply a crude irrigation system often were destroyed by floods. This changed dramatically when Elephant Butte Dam, near the town of Truth or Consequences, was completed in 1916. At the time, the dam was the largest structure to impound water ever constructed in the United States. It was the second major reclamation project in the Southwest and provided both flood control and a reliable source of irrigation water for downstream farms. Caballo Reservoir, at the northern end of the Hatch Valley, was completed in 1937 and provides both flood control and additional storage for water.

THE CLIMATE

Weather is important because chile requires lots of sunshine and warm temperatures to grow. The Hatch Valley has an average temperature of 79 degrees and almost nine inches of rainfall per year. One farmer explained that they had about as much daily sunshine as any place in the country, and because of the high desert climate with its low humidity, the area is ideal for chile cultivation.

SEEDS, THE HEART OF THE CROP

Chile is a native of the New World and was in wide use when the Spanish arrived in the late 1500s. Members of the Solanaceae (nightshade) family, the *Capsicum* species are closely related to eggplant, potato, petunia, tomato and tobacco. Columbus came to the New World looking for, in addition to gold, Asian spices such as black pepper. Believing that he had reached Asia, Columbus caused an everlasting amount of confusion by naming the native Americans "Indians" and the *Capsicum* spice "pepper."

In areas of the world that lack a killing frost, chile peppers grow year-round, with some plants in Central America reported to live ten years or more. They are annuals in the United States and require an extensive amount of cultivation. Most consumers consider chile to be a vegetable, although botanically speaking it is a berry. When chile begins to mature, it is green. When used at that stage it is eaten as a vegetable. When the pod is mature, it turns red, and is dried and ground to become a spice. According to New Mexico State University, it is the most consumed spice in the world, and probably one of the least expensive.

There are commonly considered to be two groups of peppers, pungent and nonpungent, also called hot and sweet. Sweet pepper varieties (also a major crop in the Hatch Valley) include the bell pepper, pimento and the sweet yellow wax peppers. Sweet peppers have more than twice the acreage planted in the United States than the pungent types, but the gap is closing as the pungent peppers become more popular. Chile peppers were grown on 9,200 acres in New Mexico in 1975. This has increased to almost 40,000 acres in 1993.

For the first 300 years the chile grown in New Mexico was essentially one of two varieties, colorado (red) and negro (black), with seeds being passed from family to family. The product was generally a small thin pod, suitable only for grinding into powder—which was legendary for its pungency and heat.

In 1907, New Mexico A&M (now New Mexico State University) horticulturist Fabian Garcia began to improve the chile peppers grown in the Las Cruces area. In the early 1920s he developed New Mexico 9, which established the shape of the pod and color of the chile as we know it today. He chose red as being the most marketable.

Until the early 1950s, chile was grown mostly by farmers along the Rio Grande for their own

The late Roy Nakayama, a legendary influence on the chile industry, as he appeared in 1968 with Chill Wills.

use, with a little extra for the market. Some green chile was harvested and sent to California to be canned, where it was known as Anaheim chile because it was also grown in Orange County. The canning of green chile in New Mexico was started in the late '30s with the establishment of the Mountain Pass plant south of Las Cruces.

Following the end of World War II, plant scientists at New Mexico State University began the long and difficult process of developing new varieties of chile that would become the basis for an entire industry. New Mexico 6-4, developed by Roy Harper and released for cultivation in the late 1950s, has become the most popular variety. It is considered medium-hot, high-yielding and can be used as both a green and as a red chile. Following his death, Harper's work was continued by Roy Nakayama, who developed a number of popular varieties, including Big Jim and NuMex R Naky. These varieties are considered to be mild. Big Jim is a favorite of backyard gardeners and is raised primarily for the green chile market. It is too large to process, but makes excellent chile rellenos. Big Jim produced the biggest pepper, as listed in the Guinness Book of Records.

THE GROWERS

Farmers in the Hatch Valley have been at the forefront throughout the development of the chile industry in New

Mexico. Many of the families, such as the Franzoys, Lytles and Boubets, have farmed in the valley for generations. Along with other growers, they worked from the beginning to develop chile as an industry. In return, the chile crop has helped to save the family farm in many New Mexico agricultural areas, according to the County Extension Service.

Joseph Franzoy was an immigrant from Austria. Following a career as a miner, he moved to the Hatch Valley near the village of Garfield around 1913. He and his wife homesteaded and cleared some 320 acres, and started raising vegetables for the mining camps in the southwestern part of the state. June Rutherford was the youngest of the ten Franzoy children and remembers her father raising chile—which he couldn't eat at first, because it was too hot!

She married James Lytel (Big Jim), and they were among the first farm families to raise chile as a major crop, much of which was originally exported to California for processing by the Ortega cannery. In 1950 Lytle built the first forced-air dehydrator in New Mexico, based on a similar unit he had seen on a visit to Arizona. This technological development ended the practice of hillside drying, with its losses to disease, weather and animals. It enabled large volumes of chile to be processed quickly and efficiently for the market. That original dehydrator is still running today, virtually unchanged.

Working first with Roy Harper and then Roy Nakayama, the Lytels helped to develop and started growing registered and certified seed in the early 1950s. This is an awesome responsibility because the future of the entire industry depends on the quality of the seed. To be commercially successful, the variety of chile grown must be consistent in terms of variety, size, color and taste (mild, medium or hot).

Foundation seed for a new variety is provided by New Mexico State University and is planted in a field isolated from other chile fields by at least one mile. Chile is self-pollinating, but can be cross-pollinated by insects and wind.

With a sparkle in her eye, June described the growing of chile. There are 60,000 seeds per pound, and it takes about five pounds to plant an acre. When the chile starts to grow it must be thinned or rogued very carefully, removing all rogue plants that are not perfect. They are pulled and destroyed if the leaf is the wrong shape or color, if it is not the right variety, if the blooms are not perfect, if the pods don't form correctly, or if anything else seems to be wrong.

"We grew the first nine acres of Big Jim," said June. "It was the prettiest chile I had ever seen! People from all over the valley came by wanting seed, but we couldn't harvest the crop for the seed until we got the approval from New Mexico State University. Finally, Roy Nakayama got all of the data he needed and said we could harvest the field and release the seed. The next day, there was a killing hail that beat the crop to the ground. But we got all of our workers out in the mud and saved the whole seed crop." —a very close call!"

In addition to the care taken with the growing crop, all of the farm equipment must be cleaned thoroughly to prevent cross-contamination of varieties. Seed from the first picking is white. Seed picked after the first frost is a yellow color, but it doesn't seem to make any difference. The seed is treated with bleach to control disease.

Steve Boubet, whose family has farmed in the valley for generations, teaches agricultural science in the Hatch high school. His students are typical kids, with baggy clothes, friendly smiles and dreams of the future, which for the most part don't include farming. It's just too hard to get started now.

Steve's family has raised chile for more than 50 years, at first for family use. "When I was a little kid, my dad planted five acres of chile. His friends couldn't understand what he was going to do with that much chile."

Leaning back in his chair, Steve talked about growing chile. It's not an easy crop to grow. Most people don't know that you can use a field only once every three years. The chile must be rotated with other crops such as onions, wheat or barley, cotton, corn or alfalfa. Sudan grass is also grown, mowed and plowed under. This crop rotation is necessary to rejuvenate the soil and control fungus and other diseases.

The crop cycle starts in November when a field is plowed into foot-high furrows about 40 inches apart. The rows are almost perfectly straight and contoured to be irrigated from cement-lined ditches at the edge of each field. Fields are pre-irrigated in late January or early February to moisten the soil. The field is then tilled again to lower the furrows to a few inches high. Planting takes place in late February and early March—the goal being to be finished by March 10, although some varieties may be planted through mid-April. A feast day for San Isidro, the

Chile lovers flock to the many chilehead events and displays at the Hatch Chile Festival, which occurs each year over Labor Day weekend.

Eduardo Fuss

patron saint of farmers, is held in mid-May, and the fields are blessed by the local parish priest. "One year there was a big storm the day after the blessing," said Steve with a smile, "and some of the farmers were really mad at the priest."

Considering that about 300,000 seeds per acre are planted, they must be thinned continually until there are two plants every 12 inches—which translates to 13,000 plant spaces per acre. Only the best plants are saved because the desired result is to have a field of chile that is consistent in every respect. The fields are continually tilled, building up the furrows around the growing plants to keep them from being broken by the wind. Eventually the furrow is about the same height that it was back in November. Tilling ends when the plant stems are strong enough to withstand most winds. During the months when the chile is maturing, hail, strong winds or cloudbursts can destroy a crop and are a continued threat until harvest.

"We usually have the first green chile to eat at home in mid-July, with the main harvest for green varieties taking place in the first two weeks of August. Most varieties are prolific, and there is a second picking of green. When the chile matures and turns red, it is picked and sent to dryers for processing into powder," Steve explained. "A light frost is helpful because it helps the plant to mature. The first hard freeze, that ends it."

The average farm is family-owned and about 500 acres in size. Chile is by far the best cash crop, but because fields are available only every third year, other crops are also important. With a far-off look in his eyes as the bell for the next class rang, Steve said, "Our New Mexico-style food is really good, and the popularity of chile is increasing all over the country. It's great to be a chile grower!"

Jimmy and Jo Lytle are the owners of Lytle Farms and the Hatch Chile Express mail order and gift shop. Roy Nakayama named the Big Jim chile in honor of Lytle's father, who died during the development of the variety. Lytle is an entrepreneur who speaks English and Spanish with equal ease, and can deal at the same time with a tourist wanting to buy a ristra or a packet of chile powder, and a trucker negotiating for a semi-trailer load of green chile.

"All of the chile grown for packers is contracted for before the first seed is planted," said Jimmy. "All of the folks who buy chile from a roadside stand to a grocery store get theirs from the green market which lasts from mid-August to late September."

Raising and selling chile is really an intensive management challenge. The fields must be kept disease-free, and the amount of fertilizer must be carefully calculated—different kinds and amounts for different types of soil. This can be a difficult task when there are different soils in a single field. Irrigation has to be precise—not too much. Lining up adequate labor for the harvest is critical, as is negotiating with processors and truckers for the best price.

Most people think only of the chile food varieties, but the decorative varieties are also very important, especially for the small grower. "A good portion of our profits for the year comes from the sale of ristras and wreaths and other decorative items that are handmade by my wife and me," Jim said as he looked at the dozens of designs hanging from the ceiling of the Hatch Chile Express. Along with other Southwestern artisans they have developed a nationwide market for decorative chile.

Jeanne B. Croft is a specialist with the Marketing and Development division of the New Mexico Department of Agriculture. In her office at New Mexico State University, she works with the New Mexico Food Producers and Processors Association and the New Mexico Chile Institute, helps to arrange grocery store demonstrations, provides material for cookbooks, and plans chile cookoffs and other events, all intended to help develop a larger market for the state's chile products.

There are a number of organizations promoting the use of chile. One is the International Connoisseurs of Green and Red Chile. They have a newsletter, and members all over the world. The organization was started in 1974 when there were less than 6,000 acres of chile grown in New Mexico. Today there are almost 40,000 acres, which produce annually about 55,000 tons of chile.

One of the first big promotions was held in 1975. The Connoisseurs gathered all of the fixings and took them to the House of Representatives in Washington, D.C. where they prepared a meal for about 1,200 people. The event was co-sponsored by the New Mexico congressional delegation. Senator Joseph Montoya called all of his friends in the Senate and House and made sure they attended—and it was a great party! Everyone was dancing to mariachi music and cleaning up the enchiladas and rellenos. "And the Washington media ate it up, (no pun intended)!" Jeanne said with a laugh. "Our greatest promoters have been journalists. And every story gets more people started using chile."

The word IS spreading. Several major fast-food chains are now featuring chile entrees. Chile products are available in most major grocery market chains so that cooks can find the ingredients for chile dishes. Chile cookbooks are nationwide best-sellers. Salsa products have passed catsup in popularity. Every day, more people discover how great chile is to eat!

THE FUTURE...

Well, it's crystal ball time! How about the future? With New Mexico chile gaining popularity every year, will the state be able to keep up with the demand? Will the good green and red be plentiful, or will we have to substitute inferior chile to keep us in enchiladas?

Rejoice, chileheads, there is hope!

Paul Bosland is an associate professor in the Department of Agronomy and Horticulture at New Mexico State University whose enthusiasm and excitement about chile are evident. He is continuing the work of developing new varieties of chile started by Fabian Garcia, Roy Harper and Roy Nakayama.

"New Mexico chile has a unique flavor," he said. "One of the main goals of our research is to maintain that unique taste, particularly in the green varieties." Paul explained that the chile industry has three major components—grower, processor and consumer. The grower wants a hardy plant that will withstand disease, insects, hot summer weather, and be easy to pick—the right height and pod size. The producer wants uniformity of variety, size and heat—mild, medium or hot. The consumer wants real flavor and the ability to choose the specific heat level. Consumers are becoming more sophisticated and quality-conscious, particularly in the use of green chile. They have tasted the best and they won't settle for anything less.

According to Paul, it is the consumer that dictates what developments are planned at New Mexico State University. "We are looking ahead five to seven years to develop the varieties that will insure the future of the industry. For instance, most current consumers want mild chile, but growing demand will require new varieties that are medium and hot.

"New Mexico has the well-deserved reputation of growing the premium chiles in the world—but there is growing competition from other countries." About 1,000 varieties of chile from all over the world are grown at the University in order to maintain a gene pool. This is critical for the development of new varieties.

Concentration is on five breeding programs: green varieties, red varieties, paprika (used for food coloring), cayenne (New Mexico is a major producer), and different colored ornamental varieties (very important for small growers). The goal is to give New Mexico growers and processors a three-year edge on the competition, because inevitably the seeds for the best varieties will eventually get to other countries. "In the meantime," he concluded, "the Hatch Valley will continue to be one of the best sources for really high-quality chile."

ENJOY! ENJOY!

So, if you happen to be in the lower Rio Grande Valley of New Mexico in the fall, visit the Hatch Valley and check out the harvest of New Mexico's best—maybe even the best in the world—red and green chile. Take the leisurely drive down State Roads 185 and 187, watching the harvest (and watching out for the semi-trailer trucks filled with chile on their way to canneries and markets). Stop along the way at the many farms with ristras hanging on the house and barn, with huge sacks of green chile waiting to be roasted and frozen for a season of New Mexico food at its best—the Hatch Valley's culinary gift to the world. Try an enchilada or relleno at a local restaurant; you'll love it!

As you drive home, the rich pungent smell of the chile in the back of your car will bring a smile, in anticipation of the first relleno of the season.

But don't despair if you can't get to the fresh crop. Hatch Brand Chile, available at stores all over the country, provides a superior quality replacement.

The quaint village of Hatch, New Mexico welcomes all lovers of the pungent pod.

Carlos Queral

Steak and Chile Pepper Sandwiches

This is a Southwestern adaptation of a Philadelphia favorite.

1   pound beef sirloin steak, cut ⅛- to ¼-inch thick
1   onion, cut into thin wedges
4   ounces HATCH Whole Green Chile
3   to 4 teaspoons oregano
1   tablespoon olive oil
½   lemon
¼   teaspoon salt
½   cup grated Jack cheese, optional
4   hard rolls, split, toasted

Slice the beef steaks into ½-inch-wide strips. Set aside. Cook the onion, green chile and oregano in the oil in a large nonstick frying pan over medium-high heat 3 to 4 minutes. Remove and keep warm. Add some of the beef strips to the pan and stir-fry 2 to 3 minutes. Put the strips with the onions and chile and stir-fry the remaining steak. Return the steak and vegetables to the pan, squirt in the lemon juice. Stir. Remove from heat. Season with the salt. Place an equal amount of beef mixture on the bottom half of each roll and close the sandwiches. If using the cheese, add it before you close the sandwiches, although some like to swirl it in the pan until it melts a little.

Serves 4

Chapter Two

Fiery Finger Foods

El Diablo Eggs

The addition of the jalapeño juice will surprise you. It is savory without being hot.

⅓   **cup mayonnaise**
1 to 2   **teaspoons Nacho Jalapeño juice**
1   **heaping teaspoon chopped cilantro**
8   **whole hard-boiled eggs**
2   **ounces Diced HATCH Green Chile**
½   **teaspoon oregano or chervil**
1   **teaspoon paprika**

Mix the mayonnaise with enough Nacho Jalapeño liquid to taste. Add the cilantro, oregano or chervil. Taste to correct seasonings. Don't make the prepared sauce too thin. Cut the eggs along the length and remove the hard-boiled yolks. In a bowl, mash the yolks with the Nacho Jalapeño mayonnaise and green chile. If you have a pastry bag, put the mixture in it, and squeeze the mixture back into the hollows of the whites. Otherwise, using a spoon, refill the whites as carefully as possible so as not to break them. Dust with paprika. Cover and chill for up to 2 hours. Remove from the refrigerator and allow to come to near room temperature before serving.

Serves 8

Zia Chicken Wings

15 ounces HATCH Red or Green Enchilada Sauce
¼ cup red wine vinegar
4 cloves garlic, minced
2 teaspoons oregano
1 teaspoon salt
¼ teaspoon pepper
20 chicken wings

Mix the enchilada sauce of your choice with the vinegar, garlic and oregano. Set aside for 30 minutes and taste for flavor. Add salt and pepper if desired. Marinate the wings in the enchilada sauce for 15 or 20 minutes, or long enough to allow the wings to come to room temperature. If you prefer, marinate the wings overnight in the refrigerator. Preheat the oven to broil and run the wings on a baking sheet under the broiler for 5 to 7 minutes, or until they are sizzling. Remove them and brush with more sauce. Serve piping hot.

Serves 4

Super Hot Tropical Sandwich

This sandwich is an adaptation of a Colonial Mexican dish. Called a *torta ahogada*, or *smothered sandwich* in Guadalajara, Mexico, it is sold on the streets, everywhere. It is super hot!

8 to 10 garlic cloves, minced
1   tablespoon oregano
½   teaspoon each salt and pepper
4½   pounds boneless pork butt
8   large French rolls
4   cups HATCH Hot Red Enchilada Sauce
1   cup sour cream
1   large avocado, cut into thin slices

Pre-heat the oven to 475 degrees. Combine the garlic, oregano, and a little salt and pepper. Make gashes an inch deep all over the pork butt, and fill them with the garlic mix. Rub the outside of the butt with more salt and pepper. Place in a shallow baking dish and roast for 20 minutes. Lower the heat to 350 degrees. and continue to roast until thoroughly cooked, about 2 hours 15 minutes. A meat thermometer should read 170 degrees internal temperature, indicating doneness. Remove from the oven. Allow the roast to stand for 20 minutes, to finish cooking, then carve into thin slices. Warm the rolls, slice them in half and scoop out a little bread for the filling. Spoon 2 tablespoons of the enchilada sauce over each roll. Arrange the pork slices on top. Drench each sandwich with ¼ cup more sauce. Next, dot with 1 tablespoon of sour cream. Garnish with slices of avocado and serve immediately.

Serves 8

Hotsy Cheese Fingers

This is a decorative appetizer which will get your guests' appetites jump started!

¼ teaspoon salt
¼ teaspoon baking soda
1¼ cups flour
½ cup butter
3 teaspoons ice water
¼ cup grated Parmesan cheese

Mix the salt, baking soda, and flour. Cut in the butter and mix to a lumpy consistency. Add the ice water and blend to a sponge. Roll out, cut into strips, sprinkle with the cheese and bake in a preheated 400-degree oven until golden brown, about 8 to 12 minutes.

Put the cheese fingers in a narrow jar and place on the table as a centerpiece for guests to help themselves.

Serves 6

Chile isn't the Hatch Valley's only attraction. One farmer has a yard full of ostriches; a fellow in Hatch has a world-class collection of juke boxes from the '40s and '50s, and there are a number of historical sites to be explored. The state of New Mexico maintains a number of state parks in the area with good camping facilities.

Smoked Turkey Nachos

1	bag nacho cheese-flavored tortilla chips
1½	pounds skinless turkey breast, smoked, cut in 1-inch cubes
1	tablespoon olive oil
1	cup HATCH Red Enchilada Sauce
1	teaspoon oregano
1	pinch cayenne

Place the cubed turkey into a bowl, add the olive oil and stir lightly to coat. Using a rolling pin, roll the tortilla chips in the bag, being careful not to break the bag open. Start breaking up the chips with your hand if it is easier. When the chips are a fine meal, open the bag and spoon the chip-meal into a brown paper bag. Add some of the cubed turkey, close the bag and shake well to coat. Continue until all the turkey cubes are coated. Put the coated turkey on a lightly oiled large baking sheet. Heat the oven to 400 degrees and bake 5 to 6 minutes. Meanwhile, heat the enchilada sauce, adding the oregano and cayenne to taste. Serve the turkey with toothpicks and put the sauce in a bowl for dipping.

Serves 4

Plaza Meatball Sandwich

15 ounces canned kidney beans
½ pound lean ground beef
¼ pound Colonel HATCH's Chorizo (see page 102)
¼ cup minced onion
1 garlic clove, minced
½ teaspoon salt
½ teaspoon ground cumin
½ teaspoon oregano
¼ teaspoon pepper
2 eggs

Mexican Red Sauce:
½ cup chopped onions
1 tablespoon olive oil
1⅓ cups HATCH Red Enchilada Sauce
15 ounces tomato sauce
8 French rolls

Empty the can of beans into a colander or sieve to drain. Set aside ½ cup of the whole beans. Mash the remainder with a fork. Mix the mashed beans, ground beef, chorizo, minced onion, garlic, salt, cumin, oregano, pepper, and lightly beaten eggs. Set aside momentarily. In a pot, bring the chopped onions, olive oil, enchilada sauce, whole beans and tomato sauce to a simmer for 15 minutes. Meanwhile, shape the bean and meat mixture into 1-inch meatballs. Place the meatballs on a large greased baking pan. Bake in a 375-degree oven for 20 minutes. Remove and drain of excess fat. Next, place the meatballs in the heated sauce for about 5 minutes. Split the rolls, pour lots of sauce on top and put 3 meatballs and more sauce into each roll. Close and serve immediately.

Mexican Red Sauce: Saute ½ cup chopped onion in 1 tablespoon oil. Add 1 cup enchilada sauce and 15 ounces of tomato sauce. Heat 5 minutes, stirring occasionally.

Serves 8

Green Chile and Mushroom Appetizer

The malt vinegar is the making of this dish. Wine vinegars won't do. If you can't find malt vinegar, omit it entirely.

1	pound mushrooms
4	ounces Diced HATCH Green Chile
1	tablespoon HATCH Nacho Jalapeños
½	medium onion, chopped
¾	cup wine vinegar
2	tablespoons malt vinegar
½	cup sugar
1½	tablespoons minced garlic
1	teaspoon cracked black peppercorns
4	whole cloves
4	whole allspice (sometimes called allspice berries)
2	teaspoons oregano
½	teaspoon crushed Chile Pequin
¼	cup chopped cilantro

Quickly rinse and dry the freshest button mushrooms available. De-stem them. In a bowl with a tight lid, add all the ingredients together except the mushrooms. Mix well, add the mushrooms and toss. Marinate 24 hours before serving. Store in the refrigerator for up to 3 days. Serve plain or sprinkled with chopped cilantro.

Serves 6-8

Fresh Herb Quesadillas

¾   cup HATCH Refried Beans
½   cup unflavored yogurt
½   cup chopped fresh basil
2   teaspoons olive oil
¼   teaspoon pepper, or to taste
6   6-inch flour tortillas
6   ounces grated Mozzarella cheese
½   cup Chopped HATCH Green Chile
½   cup diced red bell peppers
½   cup chopped tomatoes
½   cup chopped fresh oregano
1   avocado, sliced

Heat the beans in a pot, and simmer for 10 to 15 minutes. Remove from the heat, allow to cool a little and stir in the yogurt, basil, olive oil and pepper. Set aside, covered, to keep warm. Preheat a large, ungreased skillet for 5 minutes on medium high heat. Meanwhile, get the remaining ingredients ready to assemble the quesadillas. Put a tortilla on a flat surface and sprinkle equal amounts of cheese, green chile, bell pepper, tomato and oregano on each one. Using both hands, lower the tortilla into the skillet and place another tortilla on top. Heat the quesadilla for about 2 to 3 minutes and check the bottom tortilla for doneness. It should be just coloring. Heat in this manner until golden, another minute or less, and flip the quesadilla over with a spatula. Cook this side the same as or a little less than the first. Remove from the skillet and cut into pie-shaped wedges. Cover each piece with a slice of avocado. Serve the beans on the side, or use as a topping.

Serves 6

Southwestern Savory Sandwich

Any delicatessen meat could be used here. Particular favorites are beef, smoked ham, turkey or mortadella. Try your favorite combination.

1   teaspoon chopped fresh tarragon
2   tablespoons mayonnaise
1   whole avocado
2   tablespoons grated Gouda cheese
2   tablespoons grated Jack cheese
1   tablespoon Worcestershire sauce
1   teaspoon salt
1   teaspoon chopped onions
8   slices bread
2   ounces smoked turkey breast, in thin slices
4   HATCH Whole Green Chile

Mix the chopped tarragon with the mayonnaise, then spread on the bread. Mash the avocado and add the cheeses, Worcestershire sauce, salt and onions. Mix all together and spread on the bread. Add the turkey slices and green chile, torn in strips. Slice and serve.

Serves 2

Chile-Piñon Crab Cakes

Mix the tartar sauce and minced piñons before starting with the rest of this recipe.

1	pound fresh or canned crabmeat
1	cup fresh bread crumbs
1	egg, lightly beaten
¼	cup mayonnaise
1	tablespoon mustard
1	teaspoon Worcestershire sauce
2	tablespoons minced cilantro
¼	teaspoon white pepper
1	dash Tabasco pepper sauce
2	ounces Diced HATCH Green Chile
	corn oil
	lemon wedge, for accompaniment
¼	cup tartar sauce
1	tablespoon minced piñons

Carefully pick over crabmeat, removing any inedible shell pieces. Don't break up the crabmeat too much. Fold in the bread crumbs. In a bowl, mix the egg, mayonnaise, mustard, Worcestershire sauce, cilantro, pepper, and Tabasco. Mix in the green chile and add the crabmeat. Form the crab mixture into six patties and wrap individually in plastic wrap. Refrigerate the patties for 30 minutes to allow the patties to set. Put ¼ inch of oil into a cast iron skillet. Place over medium heat for 10 minutes. Add the crab cakes and fry 3 minutes per side, or until golden brown. Don't turn more than once. Serve immediately with lemon wedges and tartar sauce with piñons.

Serves 6

Quesadillas Quebradas

4   ounces HATCH Picante Sauce
    corn oil
8   6-inch flour tortillas
8   slices smoked turkey breast
8   ounces grated Jack cheese
2   cups shredded lettuce
1   whole tomato, sliced

Make sure the picante sauce is at room temperature. Use a microwave to bring it to room temperature or a little higher, if necessary. Pour the corn oil ¼ inch deep in a large skillet, heat over medium flame. Lay a slice of smoked turkey on each tortilla, then spread 1 heaping teaspoon of salsa. Sprinkle one-eighth of the cheese onto the tortilla. Close the tortilla firmly with toothpicks. Fry the quesadillas in the oil one at a time until golden. Remove, and drain on brown paper in a warm preheated oven. Serve the quesadillas on a bed of shredded lettuce with a tomato slice.

Serves 4

Colonel Hatch's Vegetarian Pizza

For the pizza dough:
1   cup milk
3   cups flour
2   teaspoons yeast
2   teaspoons salt
2   tablespoons olive oil

Toppings:
6   plum tomatoes, thinly sliced
1   cup chopped zucchini
¼   cup sliced scallions, green and white parts
½   pound eggplant, peeled and chopped
2   tablespoons olive oil, for brushing the pizza
4   ounces Chopped HATCH Green Chile
25   HATCH Nacho Jalapeños
⅛   teaspoon each salt and pepper
¼   cup corn meal
3   cloves garlic, minced
1   teaspoon thyme
1   teaspoon oregano
½   cup grated Parmesan cheese

To make the dough:

Place the milk in a saucepan and heat until it reaches 155 degrees. If you have a microwave with a temperature probe, put the milk into a measuring cup and heat it in your microwave to the proper temperature. Meanwhile, measure 15 ounces of flour or 3 cups into a mixer bowl. When the microwave rings that the milk is at temperature, sprinkle the yeast over the milk, stirring with a whisk or a fork to blend the yeast in. When the yeast is fully incorporated, add the salt. Blend to mix. Start the blender and pour the milk into the flour slowly. When all the milk is added, drizzle the olive oil down the side of the bowl. Using a dough hook, or by hand, knead the dough about 10 minutes. When the dough is fully kneaded, cover the bowl tightly with plastic wrap. Put a rubber band around the rim if necessary. Set the bowl in a warm place to rise and punch down 90 minutes later.

To make the pizza:

Preheat the oven to 400 to 450 degrees. Put the tomatoes, zucchini, scallions and eggplant into a roasting pan, brush a little olive oil over the vegetables, and place the pan into the preheated oven. Roast them for 5 minutes. Remove and cool enough to handle. Add the green chile and jalapeños, sprinkle with salt and pepper and mix. Remove the dough from the bowl and roll it out on a floured board. Dust the pizza baking dish with corn meal. Spread out the dough in the pizza baking dish and put the toppings on it in the following order: brush with olive oil, and sprinkle with the garlic, thyme and oregano. Layer the tomatoes, scallions, zucchini, eggplant, green chile, and nachos. Sprinkle 3 tablespoons of the Parmesan on top. Bake for 8 to 10 minutes, lifting up the crust to see if the bottom is golden brown. Remove from the oven, cut in slices and serve. Put the extra Parmesan cheese on the table so the guests may help themselves.

Serves 10

Cajun Mushrooms

This recipe was created by Mildred Brown of Mildred's VIP Catering in Jackson Mississippi, and appears courtesy of Dave DeWitt and his book, *Hot Spots—Spicy Recipes from America's Most Celebrated Fiery Foods Restaurants.*

½   **cup unsalted butter**
1   **pound fresh mushrooms, cleaned and trimmed**
3   **tablespoons HATCH Nacho Jalapeño slices, diced**
4   **tablespoons Worcestershire sauce**
1   **teaspoon lemon juice**
⅛   **cup white wine**

Saute the mushrooms in butter for 3 minutes over medium heat. Add the remaining ingredients and simmer for an additional 2 minutes. Place mushrooms and sauce in a chafing dish and serve with toothpicks.

Serves   4 to 6

House Joint Resolution 337, seeking to name chile as "America's Official Food," has been simmering since it was introduced by former New Mexico Congressman Manuel Lujan Jr. in the mid-1980s. Jim West, executive director of the International Chile Society, says enactment of the resolution is still being sought. "After all, chile was created in America by the first Americans!"

These are fresh green New Mexico chiles, the variety grown in Hatch and used in HATCH brand products.

Salsa Fria

This salsa was contributed by Kathleen Orians Dawson, who can attest to the fact that home-made salsa is always a hit at any event.

4   tomatoes, chopped
1   large onion, chopped
½   cup finely chopped celery
1   medium green or red bell pepper, chopped
2   4-ounce cans Chopped HATCH Green Chile
2   tablespoons red wine vinegar
3   tablespoons chopped fresh cilantro
1   teaspoon mustard seed
4   ounces HATCH Nacho Jalapeño slices, diced (add as much as desired)

Combine all ingredients. Chill for several hours. All ingredients may be processed in a food processor for smoother texture.

Yield: 3 cups

Chapter Three

Super Salsas and Sauces

Black Olive and Chile Pesto

This exciting variation on basil and piñon based pestos is delicious with tacos of any description. It can even be used as a rub or marinade.

½   pound whole black olives, oil cured, pits removed
1   whole fresh lemon, squeezed, optional
¼   cup olive oil
½   teaspoon oregano
4   ounces Diced HATCH Green Chile

Put the pitted olives in the processor and process briefly. Add lemon juice or olive oil (or some of both). Process to a puree. Stir the oregano and green chile in by hand. Bottle, and top off with olive oil. Use as a condiment. Will keep several weeks in the refrigerator.

Makes 1 to 2 cups

Slightly Spicy Spaghetti Sauce

3   tablespoons olive oil
½   onion, chopped
3   celery stalks, peeled and chopped
2   ounces Diced HATCH Green Chile
1   15-ounce can tomatoes
½   teaspoon paprika
¼   teaspoon salt and pepper, or to taste
4   ounces chopped ripe olives

Heat the oil in a large sauce pot. When it is nearly smoking, add the onion, celery and chiles. Saute until they wilt. Add the tomatoes, turn the heat up and break up the tomatoes with the back of a spoon. When the sauce starts to boil, reduce heat to a simmer. Add the paprika, and salt and pepper to taste. Simmer, uncovered, 20 to 30 minutes to reduce the sauce and concentrate the flavors. Run through a food mill or blender. Return to the pot to reheat. During the last 2 to 3 minutes, add the olives. This sauce will keep several days in the refrigerator.

Serves 6

When the Santa Fe trail officially opened in 1821, William Becknell of Missouri was the first trader to reach the Plaza, on November 16th. He brought pack mules loaded with goods to trade. It had been only two months prior, on September 16th, that Mexico had thrown off the yoke of Spain. If it had not been for that, Becknell would have been thrown in jail, for the Spanish Crown had expressly forbidden the crown royals to trade with foreigners.

Quick Salsa Verde

7	ounces Chopped HATCH Green Chile
1	tablespoon HATCH Nacho Jalapeños, or more to taste
1	28-ounce can of tomatoes
10	fresh cilantro leaves
3	green onions, chopped
1	tablespoon salt

Combine all the ingredients in a blender and blend briefly. Flip blender jar over to prevent salsa from becoming too watery. Refrigerate for one hour. Remove from the refrigerator thirty minutes before serving.

Makes 4 cups of salsa

Red Mesa BBQ Sauce

1   stick margarine
1   onion, chopped
1   clove garlic, mashed
1   whole lemon
1   cup HATCH Red Enchilada Sauce
1½ teaspoons Dijon mustard
½   cup vinegar
1   tablespoon brown sugar
1   tablespoon Worcestershire sauce
2   tablespoons paprika
1   teaspoon oregano
½   teaspoon salt

Heat the margarine in a sauce pot and add the onion and garlic. Saute until lightly browned. Squeeze the juice from the lemon and add with the remaining ingredients. Simmer 30 minutes. Taste and correct seasonings. Use with any grilled meat or poultry. Also makes a good marinade.

Makes 2½ cups of sauce

La Mesa Chile Sauce

40   tomatoes
5   large white onions
15   ounces HATCH Nacho Jalapeños
     water as needed
3½   cups cider vinegar
¾   cup sugar
2   tablespoons salt
5   cloves garlic
1   tablespoon oregano
2   tablespoons ground cumin
4   ounces red chile powder
1   tablespoon dry mustard

In a food processor or blender, chop the tomatoes and onions in batches. Put the puree in a stock pot. Add the nachos and a little of their juice to the blender. Blend. Add to the pot. Add sufficient water. Bring to a low boil for 2 hours. Add the vinegar, sugar, salt and garlic. Boil 1 hour longer. Stir to mix well. Next, add the spices, herbs and mustard. Stir again to thoroughly mix. Pour the salsa into sterilized, hot pint jars and seal. Matures in 2 weeks. Use within 6 months.

Makes 3½ quarts of chile sauce.

Freezer Salsa del Sol

This wonderful recipe is graciously provided through the assistance of the New Mexico State Department of Agriculture. It gets its name because it freezes well.

8   cups chopped tomatoes
2   cups chopped green tomatoes
2   cups chopped onions
3   cups Diced HATCH Green Chile
3   teaspoons oregano
2   teaspoons salt
½   teaspoon ground cumin
1   teaspoon black pepper
1   teaspoon cilantro

Combine all the ingredients in a stock pot and bring to a boil. Simmer, uncovered, for 5 minutes and set aside. When salsa reaches room temperature, put in freezer containers and freeze. Will keep 1 year, frozen. Fresh salsa kept in the refrigerator will keep 7 days.

Makes 3 quarts

Cracked Wheat Sauce for Meat

If you can't find cracked wheat at a health food store, try bulgur wheat.

2   tablespoons butter
1   medium onion, chopped
3   ounces Chopped HATCH Green Chile
2   cups cracked wheat
2   cups water
1   tablespoon Beef Stock (see page 61)
¼   teaspoon salt
⅛   teaspoon black pepper
¼   teaspoon ground cumin seeds
½   teaspoon garlic powder
½   teaspoon oregano, or to taste

Melt the butter. Saute the onion and chile together. Add the cracked wheat and saute over high heat for 3 to 5 minutes, turning and stirring constantly to coat each grain of wheat with butter. Add 2 cups of water and the remaining ingredients and simmer for 25 minutes, stirring to prevent the wheat from starting to stick or settle to the bottom of the pan. At 20 minutes, cooking time, eat a few grains. They are done when they are soft but barely moist. Use this as an accompaniment for any meat.

Serves 8

Frontier Seafood Sauce

The old Pacific and Atlantic Hotel in Albuquerque got its name from Albuquerque being considered halfway between those two oceans. Somebody's map must have been drawn by hand.

½   cup HATCH Red Enchilada Sauce
2   tablespoons prepared horseradish
½   cup ketchup
3   tablespoons lemon or lime juice
1   teaspoon salt, or to taste
½   teaspoon oregano

Mix the enchilada sauce with the other ingredients, adding up to 1 teaspoon of salt to taste. Use this sauce with any seafood.

Serves 4

The first chili championship cookoff was held in 1967 at the Chisos Oases Saloon in Terlingua, Texas. Wick Fowler and H. Allen Smith were the contestants. The cookoff was declared a tie because one judge voted for Fowler, one for Smith, and the third got drunk and forgot to vote. Today, chili cookoffs are held in almost every state, with several claiming to be the "National Championship."

Chile Guacamole

4	ounces Chopped HATCH Green Chile
2	whole avocados, mashed
1	teaspoon salt
1	small tomato, diced
½	teaspoon lemon juice, or to taste
1	clove garlic, minced
¼	cup sour cream, optional

Mix all ingredients except for the sour cream. Cover and chill, allowing 30 minutes for the flavors to blend. Remove from refrigerator and allow 20 minutes to return to near room temperature. Mix in a little sour cream for a smoother texture.

Serves 4

Mesilla Valley Molé

1   ounce Chopped HATCH Green Chile
½   cup almonds
¼   cup raisins
3   cloves garlic, minced
1   small white onion, quartered
2   tablespoons lard or shortening
1   teaspoon salt
½   cup saltine crackers, broken into crumbs
½   ounce unsweetened, grated chocolate
1   teaspoon paprika
    Santa Fe Chicken Stock, as needed to make a sauce (see page 63)
½   teaspoon anise seeds
2   cups cooked and shredded chicken

In a blender or food processor, put the chile, almonds, raisins, garlic, onion and 2 tablespoons of melted lard. Blend this to a smooth puree. Pour into a saucepan and add the remaining ingredients, except the chicken. The pan should get hot enough for the sauce to sizzle. Once it boils for 5 minutes, lower flame to a simmer and heat an additional 15 minutes. Add salt to taste. During the last 5 minutes, add the shredded or chopped chicken and heat through. The anise seeds give this dish that *authentic flavor*.

Serves   4

La Mesilla

Outside of Las Cruces is La Mesilla. La Mesilla was the Mexican border town that became part of the United States under the Gadsden Purchase in 1853. James Gadsden arranged the purchase of 45,000 square miles of Mexican territory for $10 million—a pretty good deal, as that works out to about thirty-five cents an acre. All Hatch green chile comes from the Mesilla Valley, the world's finest chile growing area.

Roasting chiles is a fall tradition in the Hatch Valley.

Mickey Krakowski

Taos Tortilla Soup

Serve this soup with lots of chips and lemon or lime wedges. Please note, this recipe requires advance preparation.

8	corn tortillas
¼	cup corn oil
1	tablespoon butter
½	medium-size onion, chopped
2	cloves garlic, crushed
4	ounces Chopped HATCH Green Chile
4	cups Chicken Stock Santa Fe (see page 63)
1	28-ounce can of tomatoes
1	tablespoon chopped cilantro
1	teaspoon oregano
1	teaspoon salt, or to taste
1	cup cooked and shredded chicken
8	ounces grated Jack cheese

Cut the corn tortillas into strips and leave them out overnight to dry. Heat the corn oil in a cast iron skillet. Fry the tortillas until golden, drain on a brown bag or paper towels, and set aside. Heat the butter and fry the chopped onion and garlic. Add the chile and fry lightly. Raise the heat and add the chicken stock and the tomatoes, breaking them up with the back of a spoon. Bring to a boil, then lower to a simmer for 10 minutes. Add the cilantro, oregano and salt. Adjust seasonings to taste. Add the shredded chicken and hold pot below a simmer for 5 minutes to warm the chicken through. Serve in warmed bowls, putting some tortilla strips in the bottom of each bowl. Top with the grated cheese.

Serves 2

Chapter Four

Spicy Soups and Stews

Clam Chowder with Charisma

½   cup breadcrumbs
1   quart canned clams, chopped
4   ounces diced salt pork
1   large onion, diced
2   tablespoons Diced HATCH Green Chile
2   teaspoons salt
2   cups canned tomatoes
2   cups of water
2   carrots, diced
2   potatoes, cubed into ¼-inch pieces
3   celery stalks, diced
½   teaspoon salt
¼   teaspoon black pepper
1   cup clam juice

Toast the breadcrumbs on a baking sheet in a 350-degree oven for 10 to 15 minutes, being careful not to burn them. While the crumbs are cooling, drain the canned clams over a sieve, reserving the liquid. Chop the clams into dime-size pieces, then set aside. Heat a soup pot and saute the bacon until it is golden brown. Add the diced onion to the pot and saute for 5 minutes. Next, add the green chile and tomatoes, breaking them up with the back of a spoon. Stir in the carrots, potatoes, celery, salt and pepper. Simmer the mixture for 60 minutes, covered. Next add the reserved clam juice. If there isn't a full cup of juice, add a little white wine to make up the difference. Place the clams in the stock pot, stir and simmer for 5 minutes. Add the breadcrumbs, stir and serve in heated bowls.

Serves 8

Sizzling Sausage Soup

If you don't have an electric crock pot, simmer the soup 2 to 3 hours on a very low flame.

1½ pounds Italian sausage, cut into ½ inch-thick slices
2   cloves garlic, minced
2   onions medium size, chopped
30   ounces canned tomatoes
30   ounces Beef Stock (see page 61)
1   teaspoon basil
½   teaspoon oregano
1   tablespoon parsley, chopped
4   ounces Chopped HATCH Green Chile
2   zucchini, thinly sliced (about ¼ inch)
1 to 2 cups water
½   cup Parmesan cheese, grated

In the skillet, brown the sausage. Drain well. Add all the ingredients except the parmesan to the crockpot; stir well. Cover and cook on low for 12 to 14 hours. Taste for seasoning. Serve with grated Parmesan.

Serves 6

Enchanted Land Lentil Soup

2   cups lentils
1   quart Beef Stock (see page 61)
1   quart bottled beer
5   slices bacon, chopped
1   large onion, chopped
1   ounce Chopped HATCH Green Chile
2   cloves garlic, minced
1   cup chopped boneless smoked ham
4   carrots, sliced
4   celery stalks, chopped
8   whole black peppercorns, cracked
1   bay leaf
1   teaspoon nutmeg
2   teaspoons rosemary
2   mild sausage links, sliced
1   teaspoon salt
1½   cups rye bread, toasted and cut for croutons
½   cup chopped cilantro or parsley

In a large bowl, soak the lentils in the beef stock and beer. Add water, if necessary, to cover the lentils by 3 inches. Pour the liquid and lentils into a large soup pot and turn on the heat to medium. Fry the bacon until crisp. Saute the onion, green chile and garlic. Add the bacon, onion, green chile and garlic to the soup pot. Bring the pot to a boil then lower to a simmer and simmer for 2 hours. Add the ham, carrots, celery, pepper, bay leaf, nutmeg, rosemary, sausage and salt. Simmer 45 to 60 minutes longer on very low flame. If the soup thickens too much, add more stock. Sprinkle with the cilantro or parsley for a garnish and serve..

Serves 3-4

Hotel Castaneda Albondigas Soup

In the 1930s, Harvey House cuisine was the finest to be found. Located at train depots, these hotel/restaurants served warm, wonderful food.

1	tablespoon margarine
4	small onions, minced
2	cloves garlic, minced
4	ounces Diced HATCH Green Chile
2	quarts Beef Stock (see page 61)
1	pound lean ground beef
½	cup masa harina
2	whole eggs
1	tablespoon marjoram
1	tablespoon minced cilantro
¼	teaspoon salt
8	flour tortillas

In a large stock pot, melt the butter and saute the onions, garlic and chile until the onion turns translucent. Add the beef stock, stir well and bring to a boil. Meanwhile, thoroughly mix the ground beef with the masa harina, eggs, marjoram, cilantro and the salt. Work the mixture into ½-inch balls. Drop the balls into the boiling stock, one or two at a time so as not to lower the stock from a boil. When all the meatballs are in the boiling stock, lower the heat and simmer for 30 minutes. Strain off any excess fat. Serve in soup bowls with flour tortillas on the side.

Serves 4

Ristras Have Been Used for Centuries

The long hanging wreaths of red chile pods are called ristras. For centuries these have been used to store dry chile for use in the home. A few pods can be taken off the ristra at a time and ground to make powder or can be reconstituted in water and pureed to make red chile sauce. Many Southwesterners feel that hanging a ristra by the front door is good luck and a sign of welcome.

Christmas Posole

Posole is the word which describes both the stew and the lime-dried white corn which is its primary ingredient. In New Mexico, a dish which contains both red and green chile is referred to as "Christmas." In addition, posole is a traditional Christmas and New Year's dish. Thanks to Nancy Gerlach and Dave DeWitt for this wonderful recipe.

For the posole:
4   Whole HATCH Green Chile, cut into quarters
8   ounces frozen posole or dry posole that has been soaked overnight
1   medium onion, chopped
1   teaspoon garlic powder
1   teaspoon dried oregano
6   cups water
1   pound pork loin, cut in 1-inch cubes

For the red chile topping:
1   cup HATCH Red Enchilada Sauce
2   teaspoons garlic powder

To Make the Posole: Combine all the ingredients, except the pork, in a pot and boil at medium heat for about 3 hours, or until the posole is tender, adding more water if necessary.

Add the pork and continue cooking for ½ hour, or until the pork is tender but not falling apart.

To Make the red chile topping: Combine the Hatch Red Enchilada Sauce with the garlic powder in a saucepan and heat thoroughly.

Serve the posole in soup bowls accompanied by warm flour tortillas. Serve the red chile topping as a garnish, along with diced onions and freshly minced cilantro. Each guest can then adjust the pungency of the posole according to individual taste.

Serves 4 to 6

Beef Stock for Southwestern Style Soups

3   pounds beef soup bones
    water to cover
2   celery stalks, peeled and sliced
1   carrot, sliced
1   onion, quartered
4   ounces Chopped HATCH Green Chile
4   quarts water
1   clove garlic, crushed
1   bay leaf
1   teaspoon thyme
½   bunch parsley, rinsed, then tied with string
½   teaspoon black peppercorns
2   cups red wine, optional

In a preheated 400-degree oven, on a cookie or baking sheet, roast the rinsed bones about 90 minutes to 2 hours. They should turn golden brown. In a stock pot, add the bones and the water to cover by 2 inches. Bring the flame to high and the pot to a boil. Once a boil is reached, lower the flame to a simmer and skim the foam which rises to the top for the first 15 to 20 minutes of the simmer. Add the remaining ingredients. Cover and simmer 8 to 12 hours. Allow the stock to cool, discard the string and any fat and it is ready to use.

Caldillo

Caldo, a broth or stew, is what the next recipe is all about. It's really not fair to call this dish a *caldillo*, or "little broth," but that's its name. Whatever it's called, this is a one-dish meal. Serve with a salad for a very complete meal.

2	pounds cubed round steak
2	teaspoons lard
6	cups water, or 3 cups water, 3 cups beer
8	ounces chopped white onions
2	tomatillos, quartered
⅛	cup cilantro leaves
2	cups Chopped HATCH Green Chile
½	cup tomato sauce
3	cloves garlic, minced
1½	teaspoons salt
1	teaspoon pepper
4	new potatoes, medium size, cubed
4	large carrots, sliced
8	large flour tortillas

In a stew pot, brown the cubed meat in hot lard. Add water and bring the pot to a boil. Reduce to a simmer and add the onion, tomatillos, cilantro, green chile, tomato sauce, garlic, and salt and pepper to taste. Simmer about 45 minutes, then add the potatoes and carrots. Continue to simmer until the vegetables are tender. Serve with warmed flour tortillas.

Serves 8

Chicken Stock Santa Fe

3   pounds chicken pieces—necks and wings
4   quarts water
2   stalks celery, peeled and sliced
1   carrot, sliced
1   onion, quartered
4   ounces Chopped HATCH Green Chile
1   clove garlic, minced
1   bay leaf
1½ teaspoons thyme
½   bunch parsley, rinsed, then tied with string
½   teaspoon white peppercorns

Place the chicken parts and the water in a stock pot. Bring the flame to high and the pot to a boil. Once a boil is reached, lower flame to a simmer and skim the scum rising to the top for the first 15 to 20 minutes of the simmer. Next, add the remaining ingredients. Cover and simmer 4 to 8 hours, skimming occasionally. Allow the stock to cool, discard the string and any fat and it is ready to use. This stock freezes beautifully.

3 C's Soup

Corn, chile and chicken make a wonderful soup!

¼   cup olive oil
2   cloves garlic, mashed
2   12-oz. cans corn
1   cup Chicken Stock Santa Fe (see page 63)
2   cups cooked, shreddedchicken
2   cups milk
1   teaspoon oregano
4   ounces Chopped HATCH Green Chile
¼   teaspoon salt
1   cup grated Jack cheese
2   teaspoons chopped cilantro

Heat the olive oil in a soup pot. Add the garlic and saute 30 seconds, moving the garlic around constantly to prevent scorching. Add the corn and saute about 2 minutes. Reduce flame, remove a cup of corn to a food processor and add the chicken stock. Puree briefly and return to the pot. Add the chicken, milk, oregano, chiles, and salt. Bring the pot to a boil; lower to a simmer for 15 minutes. Meanwhile, grate the cheese, put it in the bottom of soup bowls. When ready, pour the soup over the cheese and garnish the bowl with chopped cilantro.

Serves 4

State Fair Chile Con Carne

This recipe won first prize at the 1989 New Mexico State Fair and is a delicious version of Chile con Carne.

1	chicken
28	ounces Chopped HATCH Green Chile
28	ounces canned tomatoes (or 5 large, fresh tomatoes, peeled)
¼	cup chopped white onion
4	cloves garlic, minced
¼	teaspoon dried cilantro
¼	teaspoon crushed oregano
¼	teaspoon freshly ground cumin

Chop the chicken into serving pieces, rinse in water. Put the pieces into a pot and just cover with water. Bring the pot to a boil, lower to a simmer and skim the surface for the first 15 minutes of cooking. After 25 minutes, check for doneness. The chicken should be cooked but not mushy. Allow the chicken to cool in the broth, if you are not in a hurry. To a 3-qt. stainless steel saucepan, add the skinned and boned and shredded chicken, green chiles, canned tomatoes in their juice, and the onion, garlic, cilantro, oregano, and cumin. Bring to a boil and lower to a simmer. Simmer for 15 minutes. Taste for doneness. Serve with hot tortillas. If you want a very low-fat chile, skin the chicken before cooking.

Serves 6

Wildlife in the Hatch Valley

There is a surprising amount of wildlife in the Hatch Valley. Desert mule deer live along the bosque, or groves of trees along the Rio Grande. In the fall and winter, great flocks of sandhill cranes, snow geese, ducks, doves and Gambel quail can be found in the fields and foothills.

Palace Chicken Gumbo

Serve this dish with the Slightly Spicy Cornbread recipe from page 170 for a dynamite combination!

2½   pounds skinned chicken, cut up
8   cups water
⅛   teaspoon chili powder
⅛   teaspoon pepper
¼   cup diced onion
½   cup brown rice
¼   cup dried chopped parsley
10   ounces frozen okra
2   celery stalks, diced
3   carrots, diced
2   ounces Diced HATCH Green Chile
10   ounces frozen corn
1   pound chopped tomatoes

Cover the chicken with about 8 cups of water and simmer for 20 minutes. Turn off the heat. Remove the chicken pieces from the stock. Remove the meat from the bones and dice it. Skim the fat off the broth. Add the meat and the remaining ingredients to the broth and simmer until the rice is cooked and the vegetables are tender, approximately 60 minutes. If a thicker broth is desired, blend 2 tablespoons of water with 2 tablespoons of cornstarch and mix into the broth, heating until thickened.

Serves 6

Southwestern Classic Beef Stew

¼ pound sliced bacon
3 pounds beef round or stew beef
2 tablespoons vegetable oil
2 onions, minced
4 ounces Chopped HATCH Green Chile
2 tablespoons brandy
1½ pounds carrots, thickly sliced
4 cloves garlic, minced
1 bouquet garni, see below
3 cups dry red wine
1 cup Beef Stock (see page 61)
1 teaspoon salt, or to taste
½ teaspoon fresh ground black pepper
8 boiling potatoes

Cut the bacon slices into 1- by ¼-inch strips. In a Dutch oven, saute the bacon until lightly browned but not crisp. Remove bacon with a slotted spoon; drain on paper towels and reserve. Brown one layer of meat at a time over high heat. When one layer is browned, remove it to a bowl and keep it warm. Brown all the meat this way. Add a little vegetable oil to the pot if necessary. Saute the minced onion and green chile in a little oil until the onion is translucent. Return the beef to the Dutch oven. In a small saucepan over very low heat, warm the brandy gently. Warm the casserole with the meat, chile and onion over low heat. Pour the brandy into the casserole, warm for a minute, and carefully light it. When the flame dies down, add the reserved bacon, carrots, garlic, bouquet garni, wine, and stock. Stir and add seasonings to taste, cover, and simmer very slowly, about 2 to 2½ hours. Meanwhile, boil the potatoes in salted water until tender, about 25 to 30 minutes. When the stew is done, remove and discard the bouquet garni. Pour off the excess grease. Add the potatoes. Correct seasonings and reheat over a very low flame for a few minutes, until heated through.

To make the bouquet garni:
Put a few stalks of parsley, some thyme, a bay leaf and some black peppercorns in a cheesecloth bag. Tie up with string.

Serves 8

Classic Green Chile Stew

This is the classic green chile stew of Santa Fe. One of the most popular Southwestern dishes, it has warmed countless New Mexican diners on chilly high-desert nights.

1	pound stew meat
1	small onion, chopped
1⅓	cups Chopped HATCH Green Chile
2	cups chopped tomatoes
3	carrots, sliced
3	boiling potatoes, cubed
¼	teaspoon ground cumin
1	teaspoon salt
¼	teaspoon pepper, or to taste
2	tablespoons flour
	hot water
	heated flour tortillas

Brown the meat in a stew pot and add the onion, chile, tomato, carrots, potatoes, cumin, salt, and pepper to taste, and stir thoroughly. Sprinkle flour over the stew, and stir once or twice to coat. Add hot water to cover and put the lid on the pot. Bring to a boil and lower to a simmer for 90 minutes or until tender. Serve with the heated tortillas.

Serves 6

Although "Big Jim" chile, named after the late James Lytel, is the most famous chile, at least two other varieties have been named after men who helped with the New Mexico chile breeding program conducted by New Mexico State University. NuMex Joe E. Parker is a thicker-meated and higher-yielding New Mexico 6-4 type chile. NuMex R Naky is named in honor of the late Roy Nakayama, who helped to develop many new varieties.

Pancho Villa's Chile Con Carne

2   cups round steak, cubed
2   cups pinto beans
2   cups HATCH Red Enchilada Sauce
2   large corn tortillas per person, heated
1   onion, diced

Cube and brown the beef. While you are browning the meat, heat the beans, drained of their liquid, with the enchilada sauce. Bring to a simmer for 15 minutes. Add the browned meat and heat through, about 3 to 5 minutes. Serve in bowls with corn tortillas or corn bread, and diced onion.

Serves 4

Chile Stew del Sol

3   pounds pork shoulder
1   teaspoon salt
½   teaspoon pepper
    water as needed
2   tablespoons corn oil
1   large onion, chopped
6   cloves garlic, minced
¼   cup HATCH Nacho Jalapeños
15 ounces HATCH Red Enchilada Sauce

Rub the meat with the salt and pepper and cover with water in a large stock pot. Bring to a boil, lower to a simmer and cook, covered, until very tender. Skim the fat and set the pot aside, reserving the liquid. Remove the meat and cube. Set it aside. Heat the oil in a Dutch oven and saute the onion and garlic until they soften. Add the meat, nachos, and enchilada sauce. Cook over medium heat about 5 minutes. Take enough of the reserved meat cooking liquid to make 6 cups, then add to the pot. Cover and simmer 60 minutes. Adjust seasonings before serving.

Serves 12

New Mexican Beef Stew

½ cup vegetable oil
½ cup flour
1 teaspoon salt
¼ teaspoon pepper
2 pounds boneless stewing beef, cubed
2 quarts water
1 clove garlic, minced
4 tablespoons HATCH Red Enchilada Sauce
8 boiling onions
4 potatoes, cubed
4 carrots, chopped
1 stalk celery, chopped
1 cup chopped tomatoes

Heat the vegetable oil in a Dutch oven. Season the flour with the salt and pepper. Flour the meat, and then brown it in the hot Dutch oven. Add the water, garlic, and enchilada sauce and cook about 20 minutes, or until the beef becomes tender. Add the onions, and 20 minutes later, the remaining vegetables. Cover and simmer until the vegetables are well done, about 40 minutes.

Serves 8

Gaspacho*

This recipe was contributed by Hatch Chile Company co-owner Kathleen Orians Dawson. This chilled soup is perfect for a hot day and hungry appetites.

2   large tomatoes, chopped
1   large green pepper, chopped
1   large cucumber, peeled
2   stalks of celery, chopped
1   large onion, diced
1   whole jalapeño, de-veined, stemmed, seeds removed, chopped
6   cups tomato juice
5   tablespoons red wine vinegar
4   tablespoons olive oil
2   4-ounce cans Chopped HATCH Green Chile
1   tomato, chopped
1   small onion, chopped
1   avocado, peeled, seed removed and quartered
2   flour tortillas, cut into strips

Puree the large tomatoes, green bell pepper, cucumber, celery, large onion and jalepeno in a food processor. Pour the pureed ingredients into a large non-reactive bowl and add the tomato juice, red wine vinegar and the olive oil. Next, whisk in the green chile, tomato and onion. Chill the gaspacho overnight. To serve, place in chilled bowls and top with avocado and the tortilla strips.

Serves 4

*Please note recipe requires advance preparation.

The normally quiet town of Hatch becomes a hive of activity during chile harvest time, when workers come from far and near to bring in the crop.

Chel Beeson

Cheese and Egg Enchiladas

¼   cup corn oil
15   ounces HATCH Red Enchilada Sauce
12   corn tortillas
½   cup chopped onions
2   cups grated Jack cheese
6   fried eggs (one per diner)
15   ounces HATCH Refried Beans
1   whole tomato, chopped
1   cup shredded lettuce

Heat the oil in a skillet large enough to hold the tortillas. Heat the enchilada sauce in a skillet large enough to hold the tortillas. Dip the tortillas in the hot oil, but don't let them brown. Heat them just enough to soften them. Drain them on paper towels. Dip each tortilla in the hot enchilada sauce, lay it on a plate and fill with a sprinkling of onions and grated cheese. Fold the edges in, and from the other end, roll or fold the tortillas up. Fry an egg for each guest and put the egg on top. Serve with Hatch Refried beans, chopped tomato, and shredded lettuce, and some Spanish rice.

Serves   6

Chapter Five

Tangy Tacos, Enchanting Enchiladas, Bountiful Burritos

Enchiladas El Pueblo

The Santa Fe Gas Company was incorporated on April 9, 1879. By December 5th of that year, the first gas lights were burning in the Territory.

4   cups roughly chopped ripe olives
3   cups raisins
2   tablespoons butter
2   small yellow onions, chopped
2   cloves garlic, chopped
15 ounces HATCH Red Enchilada Sauce
¼   cup ground Chile Ancho or Chile Pasillas
1   tablespoon tarragon vinegar
1   teaspoon dried oregano
1   tablespoon brown sugar
12 large flour tortillas
1   pound grated Gouda cheese

Mix olives and raisins in a bowl, set aside. For the salsa: melt the butter, brown the onions and garlic. Stir in the enchilada sauce, ground chile, vinegar, oregano and brown sugar. Simmer 15 minutes, set aside and keep warm. Dip one tortilla at a time in the salsa. Put $\frac{1}{12}$ of the raisin-olive mixture in it. Add 1 tablespoon of the salsa and some grated cheese. Roll the tortilla up and place in a baking dish. Make remaining enchiladas. Pour remaining salsa over tortillas, top with remaining cheese, bake at 325 degrees F. for 10 to 15 minutes.

Serves 6

Chorizo and Egg Burritos

8   whole eggs
4   ounces water
15 ounces Refried Beans
1   pound Colonel Hatch's Chorizo (see page 102)
4   10-inch flour tortillas
4   ounces grated Jack cheese

Heat a large skillet for the chorizo and eggs and another to heat the tortillas. While they are heating, break the eggs into a bowl and add the water. Whisk well together. In the microwave or on the stove, heat the refried beans to a low simmer. Crumble the chorizo and add it to the preheated skillet. Fry about 5 minutes, re-whisk the eggs briefly, only 4 or 5 turns, and add them to the frying chorizo. Scramble the eggs and chorizo together. Heat the tortillas, and when the scrambled eggs are still soft, spread a layer of beans on the tortillas, followed by the scrambled eggs and a little sprinkle of cheese. Roll as for burritos. Keep in preheated oven until ready to serve.

Serves 4

Burritos con Pollo

Hatch is the chile capital of the world. That's how the Hatch Chamber of Commerce bills itself. Mexico and India produce more chile, but none better than that from the Mesilla Valley, Hatch's home.

1 tablespoon of butter or olive oil
1 pound precooked chicken pieces
1 cup HATCH Green Enchilada Sauce
8 10-inch flour tortillas
4 ounces grated Jack cheese
   shredded lettuce, for garnish
   chopped tomato, for garnish

In a skillet, heat a little oil or butter, add the de-boned chicken and fry to heat through. Add the green enchilada sauce, raise the flame to bring the skillet to a boil, lower the heat to a simmer and cover. Simmer the chicken for 15 minutes. Remove from the flame. Heat a skillet, griddle or comal to heat the tortillas on. Put the heated tortilla on a counter. Using tongs, put the chicken on the tortilla. Sprinkle on the cheese and a little more sauce. Add the lettuce and tomato. Roll up as for burritos. Put in a preheated oven and keep warm until ready to serve.

Serves 8

Turkey Enchiladas

The turkey is a native of the New World.

2   cups cooked turkey, cut in ½-inch cubes
15 ounces HATCH Red Enchilada Sauce
4   ounces Chopped HATCH Green Chile
1   teaspoon dried onion flakes
1   teaspoon dried cilantro
12 medium-size corn tortillas
    nonstick cooking spray
2   tablespoons chopped onions
1   cup chopped tomatoes
¼   cup chopped black olives
1   cup grated Parmesan cheese
2   cups shredded lettuce

In a bowl mix the turkey, ½ cup of the enchilada sauce, the chiles, onion flakes and the cilantro. Spoon 2 heaping tablespoons of the turkey mixture down the center of each tortilla. Roll the tortillas. Spray the nonstick cooking spray onto a 9" x 12" baking dish. Place the tortillas, seam side down, in the dish. Top the tortillas with remaining enchilada sauce, onions, tomato, olives and cheese. Bake in 350-degree oven 25 to 30 minutes or until the enchiladas are hot and bubbly. Heat each diner's plate in the oven. Remove the plates. Use a spatula and put the hot enchiladas on the plates and garnish with lettuce. Serve hot.

Serves 6

The U.S. Department of Energy office in Albuquerque has held an annual chile cookoff for the past ten years. All the winners in both the red and green competitions have stated that they got their recipe from their mothers.

Chicken and Blue Corn Tacos

1½ pounds skinless, boneless chicken breasts
½   cup chopped onions
2   cloves garlic, minced
1   tablespoon olive oil
5   small tomatoes, chopped
1   cup Chicken Stock Santa Fe (see page 63)
1   ounce fresh Chile Pasillas, or 1 tablespoon ground chile
½   teaspoon cumin seeds
½   teaspoon crushed oregano
1   bay leaf
1   teaspoon salt, or to taste
12 HATCH Blue Corn Taco Shells
    lettuce, shredded

Toast the cumin on a cookie sheet in the oven at 350 degrees until light brown. When the cumin has cooled, grind the seeds to a powder with a mortar and pestle. Chop the chicken as for tacos. Heat a saucepan and saute the onions and garlic in the olive oil for about 5 minutes. Add the chicken meat, tomatoes, chicken stock, chopped Chile Pasillas, cumin, oregano, bay leaf and salt to taste. Simmer this sauce for about 30 minutes, removing the excess liquid at the end of the cooking time. Don't reduce it too much, however. While the sauce is simmering, heat the oven to 375 degrees. During the last 5 to 7 minutes of sauce cooking time, heat the taco shells. Fill the shells, garnish with shredded fresh lettuce and serve. Top with extra enchilada sauce if you like tacos extra spicy.

Serves 4

Tacos Mariposa

2   slices bacon, reserving the fat
1   pound lean ground beef
1   tablespoon Diced HATCH Green Chile
2   tablespoons piñon nuts or slivered almonds
1   tablespoon minced raisins
1   tablespoon minced cilantro
1   tablespoon minced green olives
1   red delicious apple, cored and minced
2   tablespoons diced tomatoes
⅛   teaspoon cumin
¼   teaspoon oregano
12 HATCH Blue Corn Taco Shells

Fry two strips of bacon. Remove the bacon and leave the fat in the pan. Fry the lean ground beef in the bacon fat, and add the remaining ingredients. Cook 10 minutes, uncovered. Heat the tacos, spread them with the filling and serve hot.

Serves 4

Galisteo Green Chile and Pork Tacos

4   cups water
6   cups Chopped HATCH Green Chile
1   white onion, chopped
4   cloves garlic, peeled and roughly chopped
2   teaspoons salt
¼   cup oil
3   pounds pork butt
2   tablespoons masa harina
1   bunch fresh cilantro
1   whole lemon
1   bunch green onions, sliced, white part only
    HATCH Taco Shells
    shredded lettuce, for garnish
    chopped tomato, for garnish

In a blender, put 2 cups of water, 2 cups of chile, the white onion, chopped garlic and the salt. Blend to a smooth puree. Heat a Dutch oven with enough oil for the size of the piece of pork roast and brown the roast. Remove the roast to a cutting board. Drain the oil from the Dutch oven. Return the roast to the Dutch oven with the puree and cover tightly. Put the Dutch oven in a 300-degree oven for 90 minutes to 2 hours. Check the internal temperature of the butt in several places. All temperatures should register at least 150 degrees on an accurate meat thermometer. Allow the meat to cool, and when it can be safely handled, shred it into taco-size strips. Return the meat to the Dutch oven with the rest of the chile, the masa, and 1 tablespoon of minced cilantro. Bring to a simmer for 30 minutes. Juice the lemon and put the white part of the scallions into the lemon juice for at least 30 minutes before serving. Heat the taco shells, and put the meat and tacos together. Garnish with the marinated green onions, lettuce and tomato.

Serves 15

Cloudcroft Chicken Tacos

4   ounces feta cheese, soaked and crumbled
1   tablespoon olive oil
4   ounces HATCH green chiles
1   onion, chopped
2   cloves garlic, minced
1   pound cooked chicken
1   teaspoon crushed oregano
1   teaspoon paprika
1   teaspoon salt
¼   teaspoon pepper
¾   cup HATCH Green Enchilada Sauce
8   HATCH Blue Corn taco shells
1   cup shredded lettuce
1   whole tomato, diced
     sliced black olives
1   teaspoon olive oil, per taco

Crumble the feta cheese with two forks and place it in a bowl and cover with cold water. Place in the refrigerator and soak the cheese for 20 to 30 minutes, then drain it in a sieve until it is dry. This can be done in the refrigerator by putting the cheese in the sieve over a bowl and allowing it to drain. Heat a skillet with a little olive oil. Saute the green chiles, chopped onion and minced garlic about 10 minutes. Add the chicken and warm it. Add oregano, paprika, salt and pepper to taste. Taste a little chicken for seasonings. Add some enchilada sauce to taste, and cover the skillet with a heavy lid. Simmer for 15 minutes. Heat the taco shells following the instructions on the box. Stuff with the chicken, the crumbled, drained cheese, and lettuce, tomato, and a slice of black olive. Sprinkle a little olive oil onto each taco and serve warm.

Serves 4

Tacos Carne Seca

Carne Seca is jerked or dried beef.

	corn oil	½	cup HATCH Red Enchilada Sauce
4	ounces Chopped HATCH Green Chile	15	ounces HATCH Refried Beans
1	onion, chopped	8	HATCH Taco Shells
2	cloves garlic, minced	4	ounces Gouda cheese, shredded
1	package dried beef per person	1	cup shredded lettuce
½	teaspoon oregano	1	tomato, diced
1	teaspoon paprika	4	teaspoons sour cream
½	teaspoon salt	4	black olives, sliced
¼	teaspoon black pepper	4	HATCH Nacho Jalapeño Slices

Heat a skillet with a little corn oil. Saute the green chiles, chopped onion and minced garlic about 10 minutes. Add the dried beef and warm it. Add the oregano, paprika, salt and pepper to taste. Add some enchilada sauce to taste, and cover the skillet with a heavy lid. Simmer for 30 minutes. Meanwhile, heat the refried beans for 10 to 15 minutes on simmer. Heat the taco shells following the instructions on the box. Spread some frijoles on each taco, stuff with the beef and chile mixture, shredded cheese and lettuce, tomato, a little sour cream and a slice of black olive or a nacho ring.

Serves 4

Pecos Piñon Tacos

The Pecos River, which runs through Texas, gets its start in the high mountain springs of New Mexico.

1	pound lean ground beef
¼	cup chopped piñons
¼	cup corn meal
2	teaspoons crushed cumin
2	teaspoons paprika
½	cup tomato juice
15	ounces chili beans
11	ounces canned corn
1	red bell pepper, seeded, halved and sliced
12	small corn tortillas
8	HATCH Nacho Jalapeños

Mix the meat and chopped piñons with the cormeal, crushed cumin, paprika, and tomato juice. Form into 4 hamburger patties. Place them in a preheated broiler, turning once, 4 minutes per side. Meanwhile, heat the chili beans, corn and bell peppers in a saucepan. Heat the tortillas on an ungreased skillet or directly over the flame. Serve the tortillas in a paper napkin to keep them warm. Put a piñon patty on each plate with some vegetable medley and jalapeño slices.

Serves 4

The Hatch Chile Festival

Held over the Labor Day weekend since its inception in 1971, the Hatch Chile Festival has become an annual pilgrimage for many chile lovers in New Mexico, Texas and Arizona. It is a harvest celebration, a place to get an excellent meal, and an opportunity to get your yearly supply of the best green and red chile.

Enchiladas with Sour Cream

1   pound lean ground beef
¾   cup chopped onions
12 large corn tortillas
½   cup corn oil
2   cups Chicken Stock Santa Fe (See page 63)
4   teaspoons butter
¼   cup flour
4   ounces Chopped HATCH Green Chile
1   cup sour cream
8   ounces grated Jack cheese

Brown the meat and onions and drain off the fat. Set aside and keep warm. Heat the oil in a skillet large enough to hold the tortillas. Heat the chicken stock. In another saucepan, heat the butter and blend in the flour. Add the hot chicken stock, simmer and stir to thicken. When the mixture thickens, add the green chile and sour cream. Remove from the heat and stir constantly to prevent the sour cream from separating. Add enough of the sauce to the ground beef to moisten it. Dip each tortilla in the hot oil, to soften, but don't allow the tortillas to brown. Using tongs, put each hot tortilla on a plate and spoon the meat mixture down the middle of the tortilla. Sprinkle some cheese across the meat and add a little more sauce. Roll the tortillas up and set them in a casserole, seam side down. Pour the remaining sour cream mixture over all the unbaked enchiladas, sprinkle with the remaining cheese and bake in a 425-degree oven until the cheese is bubbly. Use a spatula to put the hot enchiladas onto preheated plates.

Serves 6

Burritos Embudito

Burrito, the diminutive for little donkey, is a northern Mexican *antojito* or snack. Asking at a snack bar in Guadalajara, a southern Mexican city, for a burrito, the proprietor is likely to go get you a donkey.

2	tablespoons olive oil
1	pound chopped boneless beef sirloin
2	cloves garlic, minced
1	teaspoon oregano
15	ounces HATCH Red Enchilada Sauce
8	10-inch flour tortillas
4	ounces Jack cheese, grated
2	cups HATCH Picante Sauce
1	cup shredded lettuce
1	cup chopped tomato

Heat two skillets, one for the meat, the other to warm the tortillas. When the skillet for the meat is hot, add the olive oil. When the oil is nearly smoking, add the meat and then the garlic and oregano. Saute about 5 to 10 minutes. Add the enchilada sauce and bring the pan to a boil, then lower the heat and simmer, covered, for 5 minutes. Heat the tortillas, place on a plate. Using tongs, put some meat on each tortilla, sprinkle with a little grated cheese, picante sauce to taste, and top with shredded lettuce and chopped tomato. Roll as for burritos.

Serves 8

Red chile pods air-drying on a rooftop in Hatch. The chiles are dried loose, or are tied into bunches called ristras.

Chel Beeson

Southwestern Lamb and Pasta

In the early days of Santa Fe, beef cattle were little known. Some venison was eaten but the common people's food was lamb, or more properly, mutton. It was cooked as a stew with red or green chile and some onion. One writer described the dish as being "as hot as molten lead."

1	pound boneless lamb shoulder
1	tablespoon olive oil
½	cup finely chopped onion
1	clove garlic, minced
3	cups tomato juice
¼	teaspoon salt
¼	teaspoon pepper
½	teaspoon dried basil
½	teaspoon oregano
2	cups uncooked mostaccioli
4	ounces thinly sliced zucchini
4	ounces sliced yellow squash
4	ounces Chopped HATCH Green Chile

Slice the lamb into strips ⅛-inch thick. Cook the lamb in 1 tablespoon of olive oil over medium heat until the lamb is no longer pink. Add the onion and garlic and saute for 5 minutes. Do not brown. Add the tomato juice and seasonings and simmer, covered, for 10 minutes. Add the mostaccioli and continue to cook 10 minutes longer. Stir in all the vegetables and simmer 15 minutes more or until vegetables are crisp-tender.

Serves 6

Chorizo Tostadas

The first American newspaper published in Santa Fe was printed on a press the U.S. Army brought over the Trail early in 1847. The SANTA FE REPUBLICAN, printed in both Spanish and English, debuted in September, 1847.

1   package 10-inch flour tortillas
15 ounces HATCH Refried Beans or HATCH Refried Black Beans
15 ounces HATCH Red Enchilada Sauce
8   ounces guacamole
8   ounces grated Jack cheese
8   ounces grated Longhorn cheese
1   pound Colonel Hatch's Chorizo (see page 102)
1   15-ounce can small ripe olives

You don't need every ingredient in the recipe list to make an excellent tostada here, but the more the merrier. Make the guacamole just before you are ready to use it. To assemble the tostada, put the tortillas on a round pizza pan and add a layer of beans, and then a thin layer of enchilada sauce. Next, in the center, add the guacamole, mounded to look like a small hill. Around the guacamole, sprinkle a ring of cheese. Next, make a thinner ring of the chorizo, and another ring of cheese, and dot the top with olives. You may use whole or sliced olives. Bake in a 350-degree oven for 10 minutes, or until heated thoroughly.

Serves 8

La Fonda Botaña

Starting as a modest restaurant, the Exchange Hotel is now a registered national historic landmark in Santa Fe, and is named the La Fonda Inn. This casserole-type dish is good for a party.

1	large white onion, diced
2	tablespoons vegetable oil
1½	pounds lean ground beef
7	ounces HATCH Green Enchilada Sauce
30	ounces HATCH Refried Beans
2	cups grated Jack cheese
2	cups grated Longhorn cheese
½	cup sliced green onions, white parts only
½	cup black olives
3	avocados
1	cup sour cream
2	bags tortilla chips

In a large skillet, saute the onion in oil until translucent. Add the ground beef and lightly brown it. Drain the excess grease, add the green enchilada sauce and stir. Set aside momentarily. Put a layer of refried beans in a 10 x 15 x 1½-inch glass casserole. Spread the beef over the beans. Fold the two cheeses together. Spread the cheese over the beef layer. Bake, uncovered, in a preheated 375-degree oven for 25 minutes, or until the cheese is bubbly hot. Remove from the oven and sprinkle the green onion slices and olives over the top to garnish. Mash the avocados and mix with the sour cream, adding salt to taste. Serve the Botaña with chips and the avocado mix.

Makes 64 pieces

Beef Stroganoff Santa Fe Style

2   pounds cubed round steak
1   cup flour
¼   cup butter
⅛   teaspoon garlic powder, or to taste
1   medium onion, chopped
4   ounces mushrooms, sliced
2   cups Beef Stock (see page 61)
1   tablespoon minced fresh cilantro
4   ounces Chopped HATCH Green Chile
1   cup sour cream
1   package egg noodles

Dredge the cubed beef in flour and brown in the butter. Add garlic powder to taste. Add the onion and mushrooms and saute until the mushrooms reduce a little. Add the beef stock and cilantro. Cover and simmer two hours. Add the green chile and simmer ten minutes without the lid. Remove from heat and stir in the sour cream. Serve on a bed of egg noodles, cooked according to the instructions on the package.

Serves 8

Spicy Beef and Vegetables Stir Fry

1   pound boneless round steak, trimmed of all fat
2   tablespoons dry red wine
1   tablespoon soy sauce
½   teaspoon sugar
1½ teaspoons ginger
1   tablespoon oil
2   onions, each cut into 8 wedges
½   pound fresh mushrooms, cleaned and sliced
2   celery stalks, cut diagonally in ¼-inch pieces
4   ounces Whole HATCH Green Chile
1   cup drained, sliced water chestnuts
1   tablespoon oil
2   tablespoons cornstarch
¼   cup water

Put the meat in the freezer for 20 minutes before you want to start cooking. Then prepare the meat by cutting it across the grain into 1½" strips. Prepare the marinade by mixing together the wine, soy sauce, sugar, and ginger. Marinate the meat while preparing the vegetables. Heat 1 tablespoon oil in large skillet or wok. Stir-fry the onions and mushrooms 3 minutes over medium-high heat. Add the celery and cook 1 more minute. Add the chiles and water chestnuts and cook 2 minutes. Transfer the vegetables to a warm bowl. Add the remaining tablespoon of oil to the skillet. Stir-fry the meat in the oil about 2 minutes or until it loses its pink color. Blend the cornstarch and water. Stir into the meat. Cook and stir until thickened. Return the vegetables to the skillet. Stir gently and serve at once with plain boiled rice or fried rice.

Serves 6

Beef Jambalaya Del Norte

15 ounces canned tomatoes
    water as needed
¾   pound lean ground beef
1   onion, chopped
4   ounces Chopped HATCH Green Chile
2   celery stalks, thinly sliced
2   cloves garlic, minced
1   cup rice
1   teaspoon oregano
1   teaspoon thyme
½   teaspoon salt
¼   teaspoon pepper
2   pinches cayenne pepper, or to taste

Drain the tomatoes, reserving the liquid. Add enough water to the tomato liquid to make 2 cups and set it aside. Chop the tomatoes and set them aside. Heat a large non-stick skillet with a tight-fitting lid. Add the beef and break it up, adding a little cooking oil or butter if necessary. Brown it lightly, then add the onion, green chile, celery and garlic. Cook, stirring frequently, until the vegetables are soft, about 5 minutes. Stir in the rice, chopped tomato, tomato liquid, and remaining ingredients. Bring to a boil, lower to a simmer. Cover and simmer until all liquid is absorbed, about 20 minutes. Remove from heat and let stand, covered, 5 minutes longer. Serve on warmed plates.

Serves 4

Southwest Szechuan Stir Fry

½ pound stew meat
2 teaspoons oil
1 teaspoon cornstarch
1 tablespoon grated ginger
1 clove garlic, minced
1 teaspoon soy sauce
⅓ cup water
⅔ cup thinly sliced carrots
⅔ cup thinly sliced celery
⅓ cup thinly sliced onions
2 cups broccoli, flowerets separated, stems cut in thin slices
½ cup bean sprouts
½ cup French style green beans
½ cup sliced mushrooms
⅓ cup sliced water chestnuts
¼ cup Chopped HATCH Green Chile

Brown the stew meat in a Dutch oven with 2 teaspoons of oil. Simmer for 60 minutes or until tender. Drain the meat and set aside. Mix the cornstarch, ginger, garlic, soy sauce and water in a glass measuring cup and set aside. Heat a little more oil in large frying pan with a lid. When the oil is hot, add the dry carrots, celery and onions. Cook for one minute, stirring constantly. Next, add the broccoli and cook for 2 minutes. Stir constantly; the broccoli will turn bright green. Add the soy mixture and continue cooking for one minute or until bubbly. Add the bean sprouts, French green beans, mushrooms, water chestnuts, green chiles and cooked stew meat. Reduce the heat, cover pan and cook for 2 more minutes. Serve with plain rice or Chinese noodles.

Serves 4

Too Soon Old, Too Late Smart

The late actor John Barrymore once commented that he "would like to find a stew that will give me heartburn immediately, instead of at three o'clock in the morning." It is obvious that Mr. Barrymore never heard of green chile stew.

Hacienda Stuffed Pork Chops

4   pork chops, extra-thick cut
4   tablespoons rendered bacon fat
2   tablespoons minced onions
1   cup dry bread crumbs
4   tablespoons HATCH Red or Green Enchilada Sauce
1   cup flour
1   teaspoon salt
¼   teaspoon pepper

Chile Butter:
1   tablespoon butter
2   teaspoons HATCH Red Enchilada Sauce
1   teaspoon lemon or lime juice to taste

Make a slit in the chops for the stuffing and set aside to come to room temperature. In a skillet, heat the bacon fat and fry the onions until they are translucent. Add the bread crumbs and toast them with the onions. They must be kept constantly watched, or they will burn. Add the enchilada sauce, just enough to moisten the crumbs to make a filling. Stuff the chops and securely close with a toothpick. To cook the chops, season the flour with salt and pepper to taste. Dredge the chops and fry them in bacon fat or oil 12 to 14 minutes. Remove and pour a little Chile Butter over each chop. Serve at once.

Chile Butter: Mix the Red Enchilada Sauce with a little lemon or lime juice to taste. Mix the liquid into the room temperature butter.

Serves 4

Grilled Steaks Magnifico

2   pounds beef top round steak
6   slices bacon, chopped
1   small onion, chopped
½   cup minced parsley
⅓   cup Diced HATCH Green Chile

Grill Sauce:
¼   cup red wine vinegar
1   tablespoon olive oil
1   teaspoon minced tarragon
½   teaspoon minced thyme
1½   teaspoons salt
¼   teaspoon pepper

The steak must be 1½ to 2 inches thick and from the first cut of the top round. Cut the steak along the side to make a pocket and set it aside. Fry the bacon crisp, and drain most of the fat. Use a little of the bacon fat to saute the onion until it is translucent. Stir in the parsley and green chile. Season the beef inside and out with salt and pepper. Stuff the mixture into the pocket and close with metal skewers. Cook 3 to 4 inches off medium hot coals for 30 minutes on each side, or until a meat thermometer reads 135 degrees when thrust diagonally through the meat. While grilling, brush often with the grill sauce .

Serves   6

New Mexico's Heart of Gold

Historians and other authors give credit for the founding of the Santa Fe Trail to the celebrated Spanish explorer Francisco Vasquez de Coronado. He came looking for the famed Seven Cities of Cibola, all reputed to be made of solid gold.

Glorieta Meat Loaf

1   cup bread crumbs
1   cup milk
1½ pounds lean ground beef
½   pound ground pork
½   pound boiled, ground ham
2   tablespoons diced red bell pepper, roasted and marinated
2   tablespoons minced onion
2   teaspoons red chile powder
1   teaspoon salt
2   cups HATCH Red Enchilada Sauce

Soak the bread crumbs in the milk. Drain the milk and squeeze the excess moisture from the crumbs. Add the beef, pork and ham, crumbs, bell pepper, minced onion, chile powder, and salt. Place the mixture into a loaf pan. Pour the red enchilada sauce over and bake in a preheated 350-degree oven for 60 minutes.

Serves 8

Cibola Fajitas*

1½ pounds trimmed skirt steak
¼   cup peanut oil
     juice of two limes
1   tablespoon chopped cilantro
2   cloves garlic, crushed
1   teaspoon minced HATCH Nacho Jalapeños
¼   teaspoon salt
¼   teaspoon black pepper
12 10-inch flour tortillas
1½ cups guacamole
15 ounces HATCH Refried Beans
1   cup HATCH Picante Sauce

Pound the skirt steak with flat side of a chef's knife. In a bowl large enough to hold the entire piece of meat, mix the oil, lime juice, cilantro, garlic, minced nachos, salt, and black pepper. Cover the steak with the marinade and marinate in the refrigerator overnight, turning occasionally. When your BBQ is hot and ready, remove the steak from the marinade, drain slightly back into the bowl to prevent flare-ups, and put the steak on an oiled grill. Baste occasionally with the marinade until the meat is cooked medium-well to well-done, 12 to 15 minutes. During the last few minutes of cooking, warm the tortillas. Cut the grilled steak across the grain in slices 1 inch by 3 inches. Place the slices on a well-heated metal or ovenproof platter. Put the guacamole, refried beans, picante sauce, and warm tortillas on separate serving plates.

Serves 6
*Please Note: Recipe requires advance preparation

Steve Dawson of the Hatch Brand Chile Company says that he gets several letters a week from chile lovers as far away as Saudi Arabia and countries in Europe asking that he send them Hatch chile. One fan regularly sends a $500 check and says "Send me whatever this will pay for!"

Beef Ribs in Picante Sauce

16 ounces HATCH Picante Sauce
1 tablespoon Worcestershire sauce
1 tablespoon sugar
8 ounces tomato sauce
4 pounds beef back ribs
¼ teaspoon each salt and pepper, or to taste

In a saucepan, heat the picante sauce, Worcestershire sauce, sugar and tomato sauce. Simmer until the sugar is dissolved, about 15 minutes. Rub the ribs with salt and pepper. In a shallow baking dish, put the ribs, meatiest side up, on a rack to keep them out of the pan drippings. Brush the sauce over the ribs, and roast in a 325-degree oven. Brush them every 20 minutes of roasting with more sauce. Roast about 30 minutes per pound, or insert an instant read thermometer into the meaty portion and away from the rib bones, and when it registers between 150 degrees and 160 degrees, the ribs are ready. Serve the ribs with extra sauce, warmed slightly.

Serves 8

Colonel Hatch's Empanadas

For the dough:
2   cups flour
1   teaspoon salt
⅔   cup shortening
6   tablespoons ice water

For the filling:
8   ounces Colonel HATCH's Chorizo (see page 102)
1   onion, chopped finely
4   tablespoons Chopped HATCH Green Chile
⅓   cup sour cream
2   cups Chile Guacamole (see page 52)

To make the empanada dough:
Mix the flour and salt together well. Add the shortening, using a fork or a pastry blender. Cut the shortening in as quickly as possible; that is, don't overmix. Mix in the ice water to form a crumby, mealy dough. Put the dough in the refrigerator for 30 minutes before using it. Remove when ready and roll it out to ½ inch thickness. Using a coffee cup, cut out rounds. Fill each with a little of the filling. Fold the empanada in half, moistening the edge with a wet finger. Seal and impress the edge with the tines of a fork for a decorative edge.

To make the filling:
Fry the chorizo for 5 minutes with the onion and add the green chile at the last minute. Remove from the flame and add the sour cream. Stir until the pan cools so that the sour cream does not separate. The mixture should be thick enough that it doesn't drop from a spoon too quickly. Next, preheat the oven to 400 degrees. Once all the empanadas are filled, bake them on a cookie sheet for 15 minutes. Remove from the oven when they are golden brown. Serve with guacamole.

Makes 24 empanadas

Colonel Hatch's Chorizo*

Hernando Cortez, Spanish Conquistador of Mexico in the 16th century is believed to have brought the first pigs to the new world. The Spaniards had been making a *chorizo* or sausage in the native land for some time, filling the casings with spices and a variety of meats.

½ **cup HATCH Red Enchilada Sauce**
3 **teaspoons oregano**
½ **cup dried red chiles, ground**
2½ **pounds lean ground beef, (or half beef, half pork, ground)**

Use only ground beef or beef and pork mixture in this recipe.

Mix the enchilada sauce with the oregano and ground chile. Put the meat in a large glass bowl or non-reactive pan. Cover the meat with the sauce and marinate overnight in the refrigerator. Next, pour off any excess liquid. To cook, crumble the desired amount with a fork and fry in a skillet. The chorizo may be frozen in serving size packages, or may be stuffed into sausage casings.

Makes 40 sausages
*Please Note: Recipe requires advance preparation.

Carne Adovada*

Sometimes this word is spelled adobada, the pronunciation of the Spanish V or the B being almost equivalent. Use mild, medium or hot Hatch Enchilada Sauce to taste in this easy recipe.

2½ pounds pork loin
15 ounces HATCH Red Enchilada Sauce
1   white onion, chopped
½   cup vinegar
1   teaspoon oregano

Trim all the fat from the meat and cut in bite-size cubes. Mix the Red Enchilada Sauce with the onion, vinegar and oregano. Place the meat in a glass baking dish and cover with the medium hot enchilada sauce mixture. Stir to coat each piece of meat and marinate overnight in the refrigerator. The next day, bring the meat to room temperature. Put into a preheated 425-degree oven for 90 minutes. Drain excess water from the baking dish, and bake 60 minutes longer at 325 degrees. Carne adovada should be well cooked. Add additional enchilada sauce as desired. Serve over rice, wrapped in flour tortillas, or in tacos.

Serves 10
*Please Note: Recipe requires advance preparation.

Carne Chimichangas

15 ounces HATCH Red Enchilada Sauce
3 ounces shredded dried beef
  corn oil
1 small onion, diced
1 teaspoon oregano
1 teaspoon garlic salt
8 ounces Jack cheese, grated
4 large flour tortillas
1 tomato, chopped
2 cups shredded lettuce

Heat the enchilada sauce to warm, not a simmer, and reconstitute the dried beef. Heat ¾ inch of corn oil in a skillet. In another pan, saute the onion until it is just transparent, and add the meat, oregano and garlic salt. Spread a thin layer of meat and a layer of cheese in the center of each tortilla. Fold the end and roll up, securing with toothpicks. Brown the tortillas in the hot oil, remove, place on a baking sheet and place in a preheated 350-degree oven for 10 minutes. Reheat the enchilada sauce while the tortillas are in the oven. Serve the sauce with the chimichangas. Garnish with tomato and lettuce.

Serves 4

Puerco Conquistador

This recipe is from Dan Stock. He loves to cook it because it's easy, but looks complicated, and the taste of tender pork chops with Hatch green chile can't be beat.

4	thick pork chops
2	cloves garlic, minced
4	ounces HATCH Hot Whole Green Chile
½	cup Longhorn cheese, grated
½	cup Monterey Jack cheese, grated

Preheat the oven to 375 degrees. Place the pork chops in a medium-sized cooking dish and with a small knife, make 4 to 5 punctures in each chop. Insert the minced garlic into the punctures, then place the dish in the oven and cook the pork for 45 minutes, or until the meat has turned white throughout. Remove the pork chops from the oven and place one whole green chile strip on each chop. Spread the Longhorn and Monterey Jack cheese evenly over the pork chops and then bake 5 more minutes or until melted.

Serves 4

Beef Picadillo Chile Rellenos

For the filling:

¼	cup mayonnaise
2	teaspoons HATCH Red Enchilada Sauce
1	teaspoon paprika
1½	teaspoons lemon juice
½	teaspoon each salt and pepper
¼	cup diced raisins
2	hard-boiled eggs
1	cup cooked lean ground beef
½	cup minced celery

For the rellenos:

15	ounces HATCH Picante Sauce
¼	cup water
4	whole eggs
8	Whole HATCH Green Chile
2	cups flour
1	quart corn oil, for frying

To make the filling:

Mix the mayonnaise with the enchilada sauce. Add the paprika, lemon juice, salt and pepper. Add the diced raisins. Separate the hard-boiled yolks from the whites. Crumble the yolks and mix them into the sauce until smooth. Dice the whites and fold them into the sauce. Taste for seasonings. Set aside for 20 minutes to allow flavors to blend. Mix the prepared sauce with the beef and celery.

To make the rellenos:

Heat the picante sauce to a gentle simmer over low heat. Beat the eggs lightly and set aside. Stuff the chiles with the filling and close with toothpicks. Dredge the stuffed chiles in the flour and set aside. Heat the oil to a depth of 1 inch in a heavy iron skillet. Use a thermometer to read the temperature and hold the oil at 400 degrees. Dip one chile at a time in the beaten eggs, then in more flour. Quickly lower the chile into the hot oil. Fry for one minute and turn over with a spatula. Fry one minute more and drain on paper towels in a warm oven. Add no more than one or two chiles at a time to the hot oil so as to not lower the temperature too much. When all the rellenos are made, put them on plates and cover with warmed picante sauce.

Serves 8

Albondigas

Mexicans use *albondigas* or meatballs in a special vegetable soup. Usually a meal in itself, a small salad complements the meal nicely. Green chiles in the meatballs make these albondigas unlike Italian or Swedish meatballs. Their flavor is unique.

Depending on the amount of juice in the meat, you will need more or less corn meal to make the meatballs. Start with ½ of a cup, and add more a tablespoon at a time if necessary.

½   **pound bacon**
1   **pound lean ground beef**
1   **whole egg, well beaten**
1   **onion, minced**
4   **ounces Diced HATCH Green Chile**
1   **tomato, small, minced**
½   **cup corn meal**
1   **quart water or Beef Stock (see page 61)**

Mince the bacon. Add it to the beef. Mix in the beaten egg, onion, green chiles, tomato and corn meal. Roll into balls and in boiling water, or beef stock, drop three to four meatballs at one time and boil until cooked. Remove with a slotted spoon and set aside in a warm place. When all the meatballs are cooked, season the stock to taste, even adding a little refried beans if you like.

Variation: Use a little beer mixed with water or stock to boil the meatballs in. Serve meatballs by themselves, or drop into black bean soup.
Serves 8

There are several historic and scenic places in the Hatch Valley. "Rincon" is Spanish for "corner" or "box canyon." Located five miles east of Hatch, Rincon was named because it fit in a corner formed by two mountains. It was the southern end of the Jornada del Muerto (Journey of Death). It later became a stage stop and then station when the Santa Fe Railroad came through in 1883. Rincon still looks like a typical 1880s railroad town.

The Santa Fe railroad depot in Rincon, New Mexico, one of the many historic towns in the Hatch area.

Avocados Acequia Madre

1 cup HATCH Picante Sauce
1 cup cooked and chopped chicken breast
3 large avocados
½ cup water
½ cup sliced roasted almonds

Preheat the oven to 350 degrees. Mix the picante sauce and chopped chicken in a saucepan and heat to a gentle simmer. Meanwhile, split the avocados and discard the seeds. Stuff the halves with the picante and chicken mixture and sprinkle them with the almonds. Place about ½ inch of water in a casserole and add the stuffed avocado halves. Bake for 15 minutes and serve immediately.

Serves 6

Chapter Seven

Powerful Poultry and Exotic Eggs

Truth or Consequences Turkey Breast

1	tablespoon vegetable oil
2	teaspoons paprika
½	teaspoon ground cayenne pepper
1	teaspoon ground cumin
1	teaspoon salt
1½	pounds skinless turkey breast, cut into thick slices
2	cloves garlic, minced
1	cup finely diced onion
4	ounces Diced HATCH Green Chile
¾	cup chicken broth
2	tablespoons flour
2	tablespoons water
½	cup sour cream

Heat oil in Dutch oven. Add paprika, cayenne, cumin, salt and turkey. Place the turkey breast in the oven and brown the meat on both sides. Add the garlic, onion, chiles and chicken broth. Cover and simmer 35 to 45 minutes. Remove the meat to a platter and drain the juices back into the pan, skimming the fat from the pan. Whisk together the flour and water, then stir it into the juices. Cook, stirring constantly, until thickened.

Pour the sauce over the turkey on the platter and top with the room temperature sour cream.

Serves 8

Slightly Spicy Lemon Chicken Breasts

Add more Hatch green chiles to adjust the heat level of this dish.

3	whole skinless boneless chicken breasts
2	lemons
1	tablespoon butter or margarine
1	tablespoon vegetable oil
4	ounces Chopped HATCH Green Chile
1	clove garlic, minced
⅓	cup Chicken Stock Santa Fe (see page 63)
2	teaspoons cornstarch
2	teaspoons sugar
1	tablespoon soy sauce
1	tablespoon water
½	teaspoon salt, or to taste

Cut the chicken breasts in half, then crosswise into ½-inch-wide strips. Grate the rind from one lemon and squeeze the juice. Reserve the zested rind and the juice. Halve the other lemon, and squeeze the juice from one half and add it to the reserved juice of the other. Cut the remaining lemon half in thin slices and reserve it for the garnish. In a large pan, saute the chicken breast strips on both sides in butter and oil over medium heat, removing them as they brown. When all the strips are browned, return them to the pan and mix in the green chile and garlic. Add the stock and reserved lemon juice. Bring to a boil and cover. Reduce the heat to a simmer until the chicken is just firm and opaque. This takes 5 to 6 minutes, no longer. In a small bowl blend the cornstarch, sugar, soy sauce, and the water. Add the lemon rind and the soy sauce mixture to the chicken, and bring to a boil over medium-high heat. Next, stir the sauce until it thickens. Taste and add some salt if needed. Garnish with the lemon slices.

Serves 6

The Mother of All Ditches

The old Santa Fe pioneers cut an irrigation channel through town. This channel, known as the *acequia madre* or "mother ditch" formed the basis of the water supply for the town's many residents. On the public payroll would have been a ditch-guard, whose job would have been to ensure that nobody dammed the ditch and got greedy with the water.

Spanish Omelet

This egg dish is perfect for a brunch or lunch. Add the Blue Corn Green Chile Muffins on page 157 and you'll have a fiesta for four!

2	teaspoons minced onion
7	tablespoons margarine
1¾	cups chopped tomatoes
2	tablespoons sliced mushrooms
2	teaspoons chopped capers
2	ounces diced green chile
6	tablespoons chopped black olives
½	teaspoon salt
¼	teaspoon pepper
8	whole eggs
3	tablespoons water
8	slices HATCH Nacho Jalapeños

Saute the onion in 4 tablespoons of the margarine until brown. Add the tomatoes and cook until almost dry. Next, add the mushrooms, chopped capers, green chile and chopped olives. Add salt and pepper to taste. Stir. Set aside, on a very low flame. In a medium skillet, melt 3 tablespoons of the margarine. Briskly whisk the eggs and water together and carefully pour the mixture into the sizzling margarine. Turn the heat down to low; using a fork, lift the edges of the omelet to allow the uncooked egg to run underneath. When most of the egg mixture has run off of the top, add the sauteed ingredients into the middle of the eggs. Carefully fold the omelet in half, allowing some of the uncooked mixture to run out and cook around the edge. Place the jalapeño slices on top and serve immediately.

Serves 4

Chicken with Molé Sauce

1   whole chicken, cut up in pieces
2   cups Chicken Stock Santa Fe (see page 63)
8   ounces HATCH Red Enchilada Sauce
2   ounces grated chocolate
1   teaspoon ground cumin seeds
24 almonds, peeled
1   clove garlic
1   white onion
1   heaping tablespoon shortening
1   teaspoon sesame seeds

Simmer the chicken parts in the chicken stock. Skim the foam that rises during the first fifteen minutes of cooking. Cover and simmer slowly for 60 to 90 minutes, depending on the size of the chicken. Remove the chicken and set aside in a warm place. In a blender, put ½ cup of chicken stock, then add the enchilada sauce, the chocolate, ground cumin, almonds, garlic and onion. Blend very briefly, just long enough to mix all the ingredients together. In a cast iron skillet, heat a heaping tablespoon of shortening until smoking. Add the chicken, stir once or twice to prevent sticking, and then add the sauce. Simmer until the chicken is thoroughly seasoned and the sauce has thickened up a little. If the sauce gets too thick, add a little water to thin. Sprinkle the chicken with the sesame seeds and serve.

Serves 6

Another popular historic site is the ruins of Ft. Seldon, a U.S. Army cavalry post that is part of a popular New Mexico state park south of Hatch. Troopers from the fort, established in 1864 to replace earlier outposts, protected the small settlements from Indian attacks, and provided a market for locally grown farm products.

Arroz Con Pollo

Burro Alley, in old Santa Fe, was the town's parking lot back in 1894.

2⅓   **pounds fresh skinless boneless chicken breasts**
2   **teaspoons olive oil**
8   **ounces mild Italian pork sausage, cut in 1-inch chunks**
1   **onion, chopped**
4   **ounces Chopped HATCH Green Chile**
1   **clove garlic, minced**
1   **cup long-grain rice**
1   **teaspoon crushed oregano**
½   **teaspoon paprika**
8   **ounces fresh artichoke hearts**
12   **ounces chicken broth**
¼   **cup dry sherry**
½   **teaspoon salt, or to taste**
¼   **teaspoon pepper, or to taste**

Split each chicken breast crosswise in half. Heat a large Dutch oven and add the olive oil. Add the split chicken breasts, and saute one or two at a time. Remove the sauteed breasts and put aside to keep warm. If you cook all the chicken at once, it will steam and toughen. Saute each piece about 3 minutes or until lightly golden brown. Transfer any oil to the Dutch oven, add the sausage slices, onion, green chile and garlic. Cook about 4 minutes or until the onions are softened. Stir often. Add the rice, oregano, and paprika, and stir about 1 minute or until the rice is glistening and whitens a little. Add the artichoke hearts, broth, sherry, and salt and pepper to taste. Bring to a boil for 5 minutes. Return the chicken breasts to the Dutch oven. Cover. Reduce heat and cook at a simmer about 30 minutes or until the rice is tender and liquid almost absorbed. Let stand, covered, 5 minutes. Season with salt and pepper and serve immediately.

Serves 8

Chile Marinated Chicken

1   chicken, cut up
15 ounces HATCH Red Enchilada Sauce
2   cloves garlic, minced
1   teaspoon crushed oregano
⅛   cup HATCH Nacho Jalapeños
¼   cup chopped green onions, including the tops

In a glass bowl, mix the chicken pieces and half the enchilada sauce with the garlic, oregano and jalapeños. Use an amount of jalapeño slices to your taste. Cover and refrigerate overnight, or a minimum of 4 hours at room temperature. When ready to cook the chicken, allow it to come to room temperature. Heat the BBQ grill and cook the chicken about 20 minutes. Serve with the other half of the enchilada sauce warmed gently. Sprinkle the green onions over the chicken just before serving.

Serves 4

During the 19th century in northern New Mexico, banks were nonexistent. Businesses relied on the barter system. The shops would carry the farmers and shepherds on their books until shearing time. They would be paid by the pound of wool. The wool was shipped east, to Boston.

Carne Seca and Eggs

4   ounces grated cream cheese (freeze 20 minutes, then grate)
2   ounces dried beef
2   teaspoons butter
½   cup HATCH Red Enchilada Sauce
1   cup chopped tomatoes
4   whole eggs, lightly beaten with 2 tablespoons of water

Put the cream cheese in the freezer for 20 minutes, no longer! This will allow it to be grated. Heat a cast iron skillet on medium low, but do not oil or grease it. Put the dried beef in the skillet and press down with a spatula. Turn it over and warm both sides. When it is easily pliable, put it down on a work surface, and using two forks, shred it. Next, put the butter in a saute pan or skillet and add the shredded beef and make it sizzle just a few seconds. Turn the heat down and add the sauce, grated cheese and the tomatoes. Once this simmers, stir in the beaten eggs. Cook only as long as necessary to set the eggs.

Serves   4

Chicken and Vegetable Stir Fry

A true work of Fusion Cuisine, the following borrows the best of several cultures.

½   cup High Mesa Vinaigrette (see page 142)
½   cup coarsely chopped green onions
1   pound skinless boneless chicken breasts, cut into thin strips
1   cup zucchini, washed and sliced (½-inch thick)
1   cup sliced yellow squash
1   cup sliced carrots
1   cup Chopped HATCH Green Chile
1   tablespoon crushed oregano
1   teaspoon lemon juice
1   teaspoon Dijon mustard
⅛   teaspoon pepper

To the Santa Fe Vinaigrette, add the green onions and marinate for 20 minutes. Drain them, reserving all the dressing. In a large skillet, heat the dressing and brown the chicken over medium-high heat, stirring occasionally, about 5 minutes. Add the zucchini, squash, carrots and green onions and cook, stirring constantly, about 5 minutes longer, or until chicken is done and vegetables are crisp-tender. Add the green chile and the remaining ingredients and heat through.

Serves 4

Zia Chicken Salad

¼ cup mayonnaise
2 teaspoons HATCH Red Enchilada Sauce
1 teaspoon paprika, or more to taste
1½ teaspoons lemon juice
¼ teaspoon salt
1 pinch pepper
1 dill pickle, diced
2 eggs, hard-boiled
1 cup cooked, shredded chicken
½ cup peeled and chopped celery
1 head lettuce

Mix the mayonnaise with a little of the enchilada sauce to taste. Add the paprika, lemon juice, salt and pepper to taste. Add the diced pickle. Separate the hard-boiled yolks from the whites. Crumble the yolks and mix them into the sauce until somewhat smooth. Dice the whites and fold them into the sauce. Taste for seasonings. Set aside 20 minutes for the flavors to blend. Mix the prepared sauce with the chicken and celery and serve on lettuce leaves.

Serves 4

Chicken Marengo Maximilian

12   canned white pearl onions
3   pounds roasting chicken, cut in parts
2   teaspoons salt
½   teaspoon fresh ground black pepper
¼   cup olive oil
4   tablespoons butter
1   clove garlic, minced
1   onion, sliced
5   plum tomatoes, cut in ½-inch dice
1   teaspoon crushed oregano
1   teaspoon dried basil
¼   cup brandy
1½   cups Chicken Stock Santa Fe (see page 63)
4   ounces HATCH Whole Green Chile, torn in strips
½   pound small sliced mushrooms
½   cup chopped black olives
2   tablespoons minced cilantro

The pearl onions are usually available in jars in the gourmet section of your supermarket. Season the chicken pieces with salt and pepper, and allow to warm to room temperature. In a large Dutch oven, saute the chicken legs in the olive oil and butter over medium-high heat for about 5 minutes. Next, add the breasts and brown them another 5 minutes. Now, add the garlic, sliced onion, tomatoes, oregano, basil, brandy, stock, and canned onions to the chicken. Reduce heat and simmer, uncovered, for 20 minutes. Add the green chile, mushrooms and black olives to chicken pot and simmer 10 minutes longer. Serve on a bed of rice and garnish with chopped cilantro.

Serves 6

Meet Me at Bent's Fort for Billiards

Travelers coming over the Santa Fe Trail spent at least one night at Bent's Fort. The Bent brothers built the best-stockaded edifice west of the Mississippi, and much to the surprise of the travelers, it even had a billiard table.

Chama Baked Chicken

In the northernmost part of New Mexico is the sleepy little town of Chama, where the Cumbres and Toltec Railroad resides. The 64-mile train ride is operated by the states of New Mexico and Colorado, and is a national monument.

3   tablespoons ketchup
2   tablespoons vinegar
1   tablespoon lemon juice
2   tablespoons Worcestershire sauce
2   tablespoons melted butter
1   teaspoon salt, or to taste
1   teaspoon dry mustard
4   ounces HATCH Red Enchilada Sauce
1   teaspoon paprika
¼   teaspoon cayenne
1   chicken, cut up

Mix all the ingredients except the chicken, adding more enchilada sauce to make a marinade consistency. In a large glass bowl, marinate the chicken pieces for 20 minutes. Next, on a single sheet of aluminum foil, place the chicken and pour extra sauce over, to taste. Wrap to seal the chicken pieces and sauce. Place the package on a roasting rack and place in a preheated 500-degree oven for 15 minutes. Lower temperature to 350 degrees and bake for an additional 60 minutes, or until the chicken is no longer pink near the bone.

Serves 4

Chicken à la King

During the heyday of railroad travel in this country, Harvey Houses set the standard for fine dining along the Santa Fe Railroad line. This is an original Harvey House recipe from 1910.

4   boneless, skinless chicken breasts
4   mushrooms
1   red bell pepper, stemmed, seeded, veined and chopped
4   ounces Chopped HATCH Green Chile
3   tablespoons margarine
4   egg yolks, lightly beaten
2   ounces cream, allowed to come to room temperature
½   teaspoon salt
¼   teaspoon pepper
4   ounces sherry wine
4   slices toast

Heat a nonstick saute pan or skillet. Slice the mushrooms, discarding the tough portion of their stems. Chop the red bell pepper to the same size as the green chile. Put one tablespoon of butter into the heated pan. Add the mushrooms, bell pepper and green chile. Saute for 5 minutes. Remove and keep warm. Turn the heat up, and after a moment add the remaining 2 tablespoons of margarine to the skillet. Saute the breasts, turning after a few minutes to lightly brown on all sides. Remove the breasts and keep warm in a preheated oven. Mix the eggs yolks and cream, and add to the saute pan. Add salt and pepper to taste. Bring to a simmer. Add the vegetables back to the simmering sauce. Blend and heat through. Remove from the flame and stir in the sherry. Put the chicken breasts on toast triangles and pour the sauce over them.

Serves 4

Caracas Eggs

Caracas Eggs are one of the oldest and most widely known of all Latin American dishes. Here, the recipe is brought as up to date as possible. If you need to serve 8 people, or your family are hearty eaters, just double the amounts.

15 ounces HATCH Refried Beans With Green Chile
3 ounces dried beef
1 tablespoon butter
4 ounces longhorn cheese, grated
8 ounces canned tomatoes
pepper
3 eggs, lightly beaten
corn or flour tortillas, to taste

Heat the beans and green chile in a saucepan over low flame. Heat a cast iron skillet and gently warm the dried beef. When it is well warmed, shred it on a wooden surface with two forks. Saute the shredded beef in butter. Add the cheese, and tomatoes. Add pepper to taste. Raise the flame to bring the pot to a low simmer. Stir in the lightly beaten eggs and cook until they set. Serve with hot tortillas and beans on warmed plates.

Serves 4

Chicken Kiva

Another great recipe from Kathleen Orians Dawson. This dish is wonderful accompanied with the Blue Corn Green Chile Muffins on page 157.

4	boneless, skinless chicken breasts, pressed out flat
2	4-ounce cans HATCH Whole Green Chile
4	tablespoons softened cream cheese
1	cup flour
2	teaspoons red chile powder
1	teaspoon minced garlic

On the top of each flat chicken breast spread 1 tablespoon of cream cheese. Place the whole green chile over the cheese on each breast, making sure to spread to cover the entire chicken breast. Next, roll the breast up, tucking in the ends. Secure the roll with a toothpick and set aside. On a dinner plate, mix the flour, red chile powder and garlic. Dredge each breast in the flour mixture. Spray a cookie sheet with non-sticking cooking spray and place the breasts on the sheet. Bake for 40 minutes at 350 degrees.

Serves 4

The ruins of Fort Selden, which once guarded the Hatch valley.

Carlos Queral

Seafood and Pasta Sangre de Cristo

1   cup chopped onions
2   ounces Chopped HATCH Green Chile
3   tablespoons olive oil
15 ounces canned tomatoes
1   cup HATCH Red Enchilada Sauce
1   bay leaf
¼   teaspoon each salt and pepper
½   teaspoon sugar, optional
8   ounces spaghetti
2   quarts boiling water
8   ounces cooked shark

Saute the onions and green chile in two tablespoons of oil. Add the tomatoes and enchilada sauce, bay leaf, salt and pepper to taste and optional sugar. Bring to a boil and lower to a simmer and cook 30 to 40 minutes to reduce. Meanwhile, near the end of the sauce cooking time, cook the spaghetti in the boiling water, according to the directions on the package. Just before the spaghetti is finished, add the fish to the simmering spaghetti sauce and heat through. Put the spaghetti in a bowl and twirl with the remaining oil. Add the sauce and serve. Serve with garlic toast and a green salad.

To cook the shark:
The dark band under the skin of the fresh shark will turn white upon being cooked. In a steamer, cook the meat about 8 minutes, or 1 minute for each ounce of weight. Do not let the fish touch the boiling water. Salt after steaming. Allow it to cool in the steamer. When you remove it, it may flake; that is perfectly all right.

Serves 4

Chapter Eight

Savory Seafood

Sea Bass with Sesame Chile Seasoning

1   slice lemon
4   6-ounce fillets of sea bass
¼   cup olive oil, for oiling parchment paper
    parchment paper
4   tablespoons olive oil
1   tablespoon sesame seeds
2   tablespoons chopped cilantro
3   tablespoons lemon juice
1   clove garlic, mashed
¼   cup Diced HATCH Green Chile
4   pinches salt
2   pinches pepper

Use a lemon slice to wipe the fillets clean. Oil the parchment paper. Combine the remaining ingredients, bruising the sesame seeds and cilantro together first. Put a fillet on a piece of parchment, spread one-fourth of the seasoning mixture over the fish and wrap the fish in the parchment. Put the fish in a buttered casserole and bake in a 450-degree oven for 20 minutes. Serve with rice and a green salad.

Serves 4

Spicy Santa Fe Shrimp

1   gallon water
2   tablespoons salt
1½ pounds shrimp
2   tablespoons olive oil
1   onion, chopped
3   cups peeled and chopped celery stalks,
1   cup water
2   teaspoons paprika
1   teaspoon oregano
½   teaspoon cumin
1   clove garlic, minced
4   ounces Diced HATCH Green Chile
15 ounces canned tomatoes, reserving the liquid
2   tablespoons flour

Bring a pot of salted water large enough to hold the shrimp to a boil. Add the shrimp and when the pot returns to a boil, lower to a simmer. Simmer 5 minutes, remove the shrimp and cool under cold running water. Remove the shell and dark vein. Heat the olive oil and saute the onion. Add the celery, the cup of water, spices, and garlic, along with half of the green chile and tomatoes. Cover the pot and simmer for 15 minutes. Mix the flour with some of the canned tomato liquid to form a smooth paste. Add the paste and the remaining green chile and tomatoes. Stir until the flour thickens the pot a little, about 3 to 5 minutes. Add the shrimp and reheat them gently in the sauce, about 5 minutes. Serve over a bed of rice, with a little cucumber salad.

Serves 6

The Rio Grande rises from the San Juan Mountains in southern Colorado and flows 1,885 miles, where it empties into the Gulf of Mexico at Brownsville, Texas. It is a fisherman's paradise.

Rio Grande Rainbow Trout

2   whole trout, about 1 pound each in weight
2   cups HATCH Red or Green Enchilada Sauce
½   cup thinly sliced onions
1   red or green bell pepper, stemmed, seeded and chopped

Wipe the fish with a damp cloth or lemon slice. In a bowl, mix half of the enchilada sauce, onions and bell peppers. Pour enough enchilada sauce into an oval baking dish to just cover the bottom. Put the fish in next. Barely cover the fish with the sauce, onion and pepper mixture. Bake in a preheated 450-degree oven for 15 to 20 minutes, or until the fish is white and flaky.

Serves 2

Salmon Español

Salmon is a gourmet treat—even moreso when prepared Southwestern style.

2   ounces Diced HATCH Green Chile
1   cup canned tomatoes with juice
1   small white onion, sliced
¼   teaspoon scant salt
¼   teaspoon black pepper
2   sprigs cilantro, diced
1   bay leaf, cracked
1   pound fresh salmon

Into a mixing bowl, put the green chile, tomatoes, onion, and seasonings. Put the salmon in a glass casserole and pour the mixture over and under the salmon. Next, put into a preheated 450-degree oven and bake, uncovered, for 30 minutes. Serve with boiled potatoes and broccoli or asparagus.

Serves 4

Plaza Oysters and Pasta

From the 1820s onward, Americans increasingly played a role in the life of Santa Fe. The gringos set up shops along the north side of the Plaza, and there traded their calicos and whiskey for wine or a hand of three-card monte, a tricky gambling game.

2	tablespoons margarine
2	tablespoons olive oil
1	clove garlic, minced
1	onion, finely chopped
3	tablespoons tomato paste
1	cup hot water
1	cup HATCH Red Enchilada Sauce
½	teaspoon oregano
½	teaspoon salt
¼	teaspoon black pepper
1	teaspoon sugar
8	ounces spaghetti
1	pint oysters with liquid
1	tablespoon chopped cilantro
½	cup grated Parmesan cheese

Heat the margarine and oil in a skillet. Add the garlic and onion. Saute lightly, about 5 minutes. Blend in the tomato paste, stirring well to mix. Add water, enchilada sauce, oregano, salt, pepper and sugar. Stir well and simmer for 5 minutes. Meanwhile, cook the spaghetti as per the directions on the package and drain. Add the oysters and their juice to the skillet. Cook, stirring occasionally until the edges of the oysters ruffle, only 2 to 3 minutes. Stir in chopped cilantro. Pour half of the oyster mixture over the pasta and toss. Serve the remaining sauce over the pasta. Serve the Parmesan cheese on the side.

Serves 6

Pecos Fish Fillets in Spicy Sauce

1   onion, half, sliced in rings, the other half chopped
4   ounces Chopped HATCH Green Chile
1   clove garlic, minced
2   tablespoons butter
2   tablespoons flour
½   teaspoon salt
1   tablespoon chile powder
1   cup crushed tomatoes
1   cup Chicken Stock Santa Fe (see page 63), or water
2   pounds firm fish fillets

Saute the chopped half of the onion, green chile, and garlic in the melted butter. Add the flour, salt, and chile powder and stir until creamy. Add the tomatoes and stock and simmer until the sauce thickens. Wipe the fillets with a damp cloth or slice of lemon. In a glass casserole, put enough sauce to barely cover the bottom of the dish. Put the fillets on top of that. Pour the remaining sauce over the fillets and dress with the onion slices. Bake in a preheated 400-degree oven about 10 minutes per pound of fish.

Serves 4

Nature at Balance

The Pecos Mission Church, built in 1635, is one of the oldest ecclesiastical buildings in New Mexico. The Mission is now a national monument and has a small garden, where a visitor can view the Indian style of planting. Together in a mound are planted corn, squash and beans. The corn serves as a pole for the beans, the squash returns nutrients to the soil that the corn takes out, and the corn gives nutrients to the soil for the squash.

Paella on the Desert

Use this recipe for a party! You can use a large Chinese wok, if it has a close fitting lid.

1	chicken, 3½ lbs., cut into 8 pieces
1	teaspoon salt
½	teaspoon black pepper
1	teaspoon oregano
4	cups Chicken Stock Santa Fe (see page 63)
¼	gram saffron threads
4	tablespoons olive oil
½	pound Colonel Hatch's Chorizo (see page 102)
2	onions, diced
3	cloves garlic, minced
4	tomatoes, diced
4	ounces Diced HATCH Green Chile
2	cups uncooked long-grain rice
1	pound fresh peas, or a 10-oz. package of frozen spring peas
1	pound large shrimp, shelled
½	pound clams, in the shell, washed
½	pound mussels, in the shell, washed

Wash the chicken pieces and pat dry with a paper towel. Season the pieces with salt, black pepper, and oregano. Let the pieces stand for 30 minutes to allow the flavors to be absorbed. Meanwhile, in a medium saucepan, heat the stock and add the saffron, then turn off heat and set aside. In a 6-quart Dutch oven, saute the chicken in the olive oil over medium heat until golden brown, about 8 minutes. Turn the pieces and brown an additional 5 minutes. Remove the parts to a paper-towel-lined baking pan. Add the sausages to the Dutch oven and brown, turning to cook all sides, for about 5 minutes. Remove the sausages to the baking sheet. When cool enough to touch, cut the sausages in half. Add the onions and garlic to the Dutch oven and saute 5 minutes. Add the tomatoes, green chile, rice, reserved chicken, and stock to cover and bring to a boil, then lower to a simmer for 20 minutes. Add the halved sausages, peas, and shrimp. Stir to mix well. Cover and simmer 10 minutes. Add the clams and mussels. Cover and simmer 15 minutes longer. Fluff the rice and serve immediately on heated plates.

Serves 8

Army Life Was Not Like the Movies

Army life was hard at best, and the living conditions at many of the frontier outposts were miserable. During an inspection trip following the Civil War, General William Tecumseh Sherman said in a report that "We should have another war with Mexico and force them to take the Territory (New Mexico) back!"

Oriental Steamed Fish with Chiles

12   ounces firm white fish fillets
½   teaspoon pepper, or to taste
2   teaspoons cornstarch
2   teaspoons soy sauce
2   teaspoons Chinese rice wine
1   tablespoon finely chopped green onions
¼   teaspoon finely minced ginger root
1   clove garlic
4   ounces Diced HATCH Green Chile

Cut the fish lengthwise into 2-inch strips. Sprinkle with pepper to taste. Mix the cornstarch, soy sauce and wine in a bowl, drop in the fish and mix together using your hand. Arrange the fish strips in a shallow dish and sprinkle with the onions, ginger, garlic and green chile. To steam, place a low rack or trivet in the bottom of a 12-inch skillet with a tight-fitting lid. Pour water into the bottom of the pan, and bring to boil. Place the plate of fish on the rack. Cover and steam 10 to 15 minutes or until fish is cooked. Serve with vegetable or pork fried rice.

Serves 4

Chiles Rellenos con Camarones

This unusual filling for chile rellenos is truly a gourmet item. If you like a stiff filling, chop the shrimp to a paste in the food processor.

3	tablespoons peeled and chopped celery stalks
3	tablespoons butter
2	whole eggs, beaten
1	cup bread crumbs
½	cup milk
1	teaspoon salt
¼	teaspoon black pepper
1	tablespoon Worcestershire sauce
2	cups cooked bay shrimp
6	HATCH green chiles, whole

Saute the celery in butter for three minutes. Meanwhile, combine the eggs, bread crumbs, milk, salt, pepper, and Worcestershire sauce. Add the sauteed celery and shrimp and stir to mix well. Stuff the mixture into the whole chiles and seal with toothpicks if necessary. Place them in a deep, lightly buttered casserole dish, seam side down. Cover the dish and bake in a 350-degree oven for 20 to 25 minutes or until heated through. Remove to heated plates and serve with beans and rice.

Serves 3

Sizzling Seafood Fajitas

1   clove garlic, minced
⅛   teaspoon paprika
⅛   teaspoon pepper
1   tablespoon lime juice
¼   teaspoon cayenne
2   teaspoons Worcestershire sauce
1½   pounds any firm, white fish fillets
2   tablespoons olive oil
1   red onion, sliced
4   ounces Chopped HATCH Green Chile
4   ounces red bell pepper, roasted and marinated, drained and chopped
½   teaspoon salt, or to taste
¼   teaspoon black pepper, or to taste
8   large flour tortillas
1   cup HATCH Picante Sauce
¾   cup guacamole
½   cup grated jack cheese

Mix the garlic, paprika, pepper, lime juice, cayenne and Worcestershire sauce. Marinate the fish fillets in this for 30 minutes in the refrigerator. Preheat the olive oil in a large frying pan on medium heat. Saute the onion, for 5 minutes, add the green chile and bell pepper and cook until just heated through. Season with salt and pepper. Place the chile, bell pepper and onion on a serving dish. Keep warm in a preheated oven. Remove the fish fillets from the marinade and cook them in the preheated frying pan on medium heat until the fish flakes easily with a fork, between 5 and 10 minutes. Place the fried fish in the preheated serving dish and toss with the chile, bell pepper and onion. Serve with tortillas, picante sauce, guacamole and grated cheese.

Serves 4

Barbecued Flounder in Spicy Mirepoix

The Concord Stagecoach Company operated between Missouri and Santa Fe. After the early years, the Company put stations along the route for the comfort of their passengers. Passengers were required to partake of the fare or go hungry. One of the passengers described the liquid fare as follows: "a vile decoction called, through courtesy, 'coffee' was served... but God help the man who disputed it."

1	whole lemon
4	8-ounce flounder fillets
3	tablespoons butter
3	tablespoons olive oil
2	Japanese eggplants, in ½-inch dice, to equal about a cupful
¼	cup Diced HATCH Green Chile
¼	cup chopped green onions, white and green parts
2	cloves garlic, mashed
1	cup diced tomatoes
½	cup white wine
½	teaspoon salt
¼	teaspoon pepper
1	tablespoon cilantro, chopped

Slice the lemon in half and juice it. Using the remaining lemon half, wipe the fillets and set them aside. In a saute pan, gently heat 1 tablespoon each of the butter and olive oil. Stir. Set aside, and when cool, dip the fillets into the pan one at a time, to coat all sides thoroughly. Put the fillets on a plate. Preheat the barbecue grill. In the remaining oil and butter, saute the diced eggplant and green chile about 5 minutes. Add the green onions, garlic and tomatoes. Saute 2 minutes longer. Add the wine and bring to a boil. Break up the tomatoes with a spoon. Lower the heat and simmer 10 minutes longer. Add salt and pepper and taste for seasonings. Oil the barbecue grill

June Rutherford, a grandmother who has spent her life in the valley, remembers that "When one of the children got married, Dad would give them 35 acres, a team of horses, a cow and calf, and 12 chickens. He expected to be repaid the cost of the land, but it was a great way to get started in farming!"

with a brush or put the fillets in an oiled, hinged wire fish basket and grill 4 to 5 minutes per side. Remove to a heated serving platter. Stir the lemon juice into the saute pan mixture, stir and spoon the mirepoix over the fish. Garnish with a sprinkling of cilantro.

Serves 4

Seviche Caliente*

This dish is believed to have been invented in the Philippine Islands. During the 18th century, Spanish galleons took Mexican chiles to the islands. The Filipinos found a good use for fish and chiles, as follows.

10	limes
2	lemons, optional
1	pound firm white fish
1	large tomato, chopped
½	cup chopped black olives
2	teaspoons hand-crushed oregano
½	medium red onion, chopped
¼	cup HATCH Nacho Jalapeño slices
½	cup olive oil
½	teaspoon salt
¼	teaspoon coarsely ground black pepper
2	tablespoons finely chopped cilantro

Juice the limes and one of the lemons. Reserve the other lemon for garnish. Strain the juice through a sieve and discard the pulp. Chop the fish finely. Any firm-fleshed fish, white in color, will work for this dish. Put the fish in a glass bowl. Pour the juice over the fish. Cover and refrigerate overnight. Remove when ready to prepare and drain the fish in a colander or sieve. When it is thoroughly drained, add all the remaining ingredients in the order given in the ingredients list, lightly tossing after each addition. Be sparing with the olive oil, however. You want to coat the fish, but not have it dripping with oil.

Serves 4

*Please Note: Recipe requires advance preparation.

To assure the quality of Hatch chiles, the crop is carefully harvested by hand. This Mexican migrant worker is picking red chile pods which have been allowed to ripen and dry on the plant.

C. E. Mitchell

Cheddar and Chile Salad Dressing

This recipe for salad dressing will dress a potato salad nicely, provide a dip for raw appetizer vegetables, and can also be used over cooked green beans.

¼ cup unflavored yogurt
1 cup cottage cheese
1 cup canned green beans
2 tablespoons condensed milk
½ cup grated sharp cheddar
2 tablespoons HATCH Nacho Jalapeño juice
1 tablespoon HATCH Nacho Jalapeños
¼ teaspoon salt
1 pinch pepper
2 tablespoons onion juice

Put the yogurt and cottage cheese in a sieve and drain over a bowl, overnight in the refrigerator or for at least 4 hours. Stir the mixture in the sieve to help it drain.

In a blender jar put half of the green beans and all the other ingredients. Blend to a puree. Add the remaining beans and blend minimally to chop the beans without making them a puree. This dressing should have a little *chunkiness* to it.

Makes 1-2 cups of dressing

Chapter Nine

Sultry Salads and Dressings

Avocado Salad Dressing

This is an adaptation of a recipe in *Hot & Spicy & Meatless*, by Dave and Mary Jane DeWitt and Melissa Stock. I thank them for the usage.

1   peeled avocado
2   tablespoons white wine vinegar
¼   cup water
½   cup sour cream
2   tablespoons cilantro
¼   teaspoon salt
1   teaspoon sugar, optional
1   clove garlic, minced
1   teaspoon HATCH Nacho Jalapeños

Peel the avocado. Mince the jalapeños and place this and all the other ingredients, including the avocado, in a food processor or blender. Blend 60 seconds. Set aside for the flavors to blend and use immediately. Variation: if the jalapeño is too spicy, use only a tablespoon or less of the Hatch Nacho Jalapeño juice from the can.

Makes 1-2 cups of dressing

Southwestern Rancho Salad Dressing

2 tablespoons HATCH Nacho jalapeños
1 cup low-fat buttermilk
⅓ cup chopped cucumber
3 green onions, whites only, chopped
1 tablespoon Dijon mustard
2 tablespoons chopped cilantro
2 teaspoons lemon or lime juice
½ teaspoon dill weed
1 pinch of pepper

Mince the jalapeños and mix all the ingredients in a bowl. Whisk to a salad dressing consistency.

Makes 1-2 cups of dressing

High Mesa Vinaigrette

1   **tablespoon Nacho Jalapeño juice**
1   **teaspoon mustard**
⅛   **teaspoon oregano**
⅛   **teaspoon basil**
3   **tablespoons olive oil**
     salt and pepper to taste

In a small bowl, mix the Nacho Jalapeño juice with the prepared mustard. Add the spices and seasonings and whisk well. Taste. Correct seasonings. Next, add about ½ teaspoon of the oil. Whisk until the oil is fully mixed into the liquid. Add the remaining oil, a little at a time, to easily emulsify the dressing. Serve over salad, asparagus, or use as a sandwich spread with cold cuts.

Serves 4

Taos Tabouleh Salad

Throw in some chopped piñons for a tasty variation.

2	bunches Italian flat-leaf parsley, minced
1	cup bulgur wheat
1	red bell pepper, minced
4	tablespoons Chopped HATCH Green Chile
2	bunches scallions, roughly chopped, white and green mixed
2	tablespoons coarsely chopped fresh mint
¼	cup olive oil
¼	cup lemon juice, reserving the zest
1	teaspoon salt
¼	teaspoon pepper
4	tomatoes, chopped
1	head Romaine lettuce leaves

Rinse and drain the parsley several hours ahead. It must be thoroughly dry before mincing. Soak the bulgur in water to completely cover for at least 15 minutes. Drain and place in a dish towel, squeeze dry. Mix the finely minced parsley, bell pepper, green chile, scallions, and mint together with the bulgur. In a separate bowl, mix the olive oil, lemon juice, zest and salt and pepper and whisk until smooth. Add the bulgur mixture, and combine thoroughly in the mixing bowl. Fold in the tomatoes. Serve immediately on lettuce leaves.

Serves 6

Drying Chile, the Color of the Harvest

Up until the early 1960s, most of the chile was harvested when it was red on the vine, and was set out to dry on the hillsides surrounding the valley. The drying chile was also hung from houses in ristras, or pods strung on a string. Many people would take the long dusty drive along the Rio Grande just to see the hillsides and houses covered by the drying chile. Post cards showing the drying chile are collectors' items today.

Smoky Hot Piñon and Turkey Salad

During *fandangos*, or dances, it was the custom of the Santa Fe ladies to attempt a *coup d'etat* of sorts. The women, armed with eggshells filled with eau de cologne, would attempt to break the shells over the heads of those men they might be interested in. If the man was able to catch up to the female perpetrator before she was able to retake her seat, he would be entitled to a kiss.

¼   cup sour cream
½   cup coarsely chopped piñons
1   cup HATCH Picante Sauce
1   teaspoon grated lime peel
2   tablespoons fresh lime juice
1   head iceberg lettuce
8   HATCH Blue Corn taco shells
1   pound smoked turkey breast
1   pound chopped tomatoes
4   ounces Chopped HATCH Green Chile

Mix sour cream, piñons (reserving 2 tablespoons for a topping garnish), picante sauce, lime peel and juice. Set aside for 20 minutes for flavors to blend. Shred lettuce and arrange it on four plates. Stand 2 taco shells upright in the center of each bed of lettuce. Shred the turkey, toss with the tomatoes, green chiles, and the prepared dressing. Fill the shells with the mixture. Top with a dollop of sour cream and chopped piñons.

Serves 4

Pecos Potato Salad

3 cups red potatoes, cooked, peeled and diced
4 bacon slices, cooked and chopped
½ cup marinated and chopped red bell peppers
1 teaspoon oregano, or more, to taste
½ bunch cilantro or parsley, chopped
1¼ cups HATCH Picante sauce

Boil the potatoes in their skins for 20 to 30 minutes, until a fork goes to the center of the potato easily. Drain and rinse under cold water. Do not peel until ready to make the salad. Peel and cube the potatoes; add the chopped bacon, bell pepper, oregano and chopped cilantro and toss gently. Fold in the picante sauce and chill 20 to 30 minutes before serving.

Serves 6

Francisco Pancho Villa's real name was Doroteo Arango. His adopted name was that of his paternal grandfather, Don Jesús Villa. Pancho was born in 1878 in the state of Durango, Mexico. While he was an outlaw, he eventually became a leader in the Mexican Revolution of 1910.

Nopales Montezuma

This dish, using the pad (or leaf) of the nopal cactus, may sound strange to you if you have never tried it. It is delicious. Look for the cactus in 15-ounce and larger jars in the Mexican foods section of your supermarket.

15   ounces nopales cactus pieces
4   ounces Chopped HATCH Green Chile
4   bacon slices
1   onion, chopped
2   tomatoes, peeled and chopped
¼   teaspoon salt
1   pinch pepper
1   tablespoon chopped cilantro
½   cup crumbled feta cheese

Drain and rinse the bottle of nopales and can of chiles. Fry the bacon until almost crisp and remove and drain it. Chop and set aside. Reserve the rendered fat and fry the onion until translucent. Add the nopales and chopped chile. Heat through; return the chopped bacon and tomatoes. Add salt and pepper to taste. Fry long enough to reduce the tomato liquid to thicken. Remove from the heat, sprinkle with cilantro. Stir to mix. Sprinkle the cheese on top. Serve *"al tiempo,"* that is, at a warm temperature.

Serves 4

Hatch Savory Salad

1	cup elbow macaroni
½	cup mayonnaise
½	cup unflavored yogurt
3	tablespoons lime juice
1	teaspoon crushed cumin
½	teaspoon salt
1	cup chopped green bell peppers
1	cup chopped red bell peppers
½	cup chopped green onions
2 to 4	tablespoons HATCH Nacho Jalapeños
16	ounces canned black beans, rinsed, drained
2	tablespoons cilantro, chopped

Cook the macaroni according to the instructions on the package. Rinse in cold water and set aside to drain. In a bowl, combine mayonnaise, yogurt, lime juice, cumin and salt. Add the remaining ingredients, including the macaroni. Toss to coat. Refrigerate 1 hour before serving.

Serves 8

Most growers can go into a field and tell whether the chile is hot or mild. Hot has a narrower leaf with a darker green color. The mild varieties have a somewhat broader leaf that is lighter in color. The proof is to bite into the chile pod. Most of the farmers carry chewing gum to cool their mouths down.

Adobe Bean Salad

In 1846, the Adobe Palace, or as we now call it, the Governor's Palace, is said to have been the only building in New Mexico with glass windows. The amount of overland trade along the Santa Fe Trail that year was $1,752,259.00.

1	large tomato, peeled and diced
2	ounces Diced HATCH Green Chile
½	cup peeled and chopped celery stalks
1	cup canned pinto beans, rinsed
1	tablespoon minced onions
2	tablespoons HATCH Red Enchilada Sauce
4	large lettuce leaves

Mix the ingredients, adding more enchilada sauce to taste. Serve on lettuce leaves.

Serves 4

Avocado and Chile Salad

¼ cup sherry vinegar
½ clove garlic, minced
½ cup chopped fresh basil
2 tablespoons olive oil
1 15-ounce jar marinated red bell peppers
16 ounces Chopped HATCH Green Chile
15 ounces canned corn
2 tablespoons coarsely chopped walnuts
12 lettuce leaves
1 avocado, peeled, sliced
¼ teaspoon salt, or to taste
⅛ teaspoon black pepper, or to taste

Combine the vinegar, garlic and basil in a measuring cup. Set aside 20 minutes to blend the flavors. Make a vinaigrette by adding 1 tablespoon of oil to the cup and whisking briskly to blend the oil and vinegar. Blend in the remaining oil. Set aside 10 minutes longer. Chop the red bell pepper into the same size pieces as the green chile. Put those ingredients into a bowl large enough to accommodate all the salad ingredients. Add the corn to the mixture in the bowl; stir briefly.

To serve, separate the lettuce leaves, put the salad on top and garnish with a slice of avocado and top with the walnuts. Add salt and pepper to taste.

Serves 6

Dr. Paul Bosland, Professor of Agronomy and Horticulture at New Mexico State University discusses different New Mexico chile pepper pod types with some Hatch growers.

Paul Bosland

Lamb Taco Casserole

1   tablespoon olive oil
1   clove garlic, minced
1   pound boneless leg or shoulder of lamb, cut in ⅛-inch strips
1   cup Beef Stock (see page 61)
1   cup HATCH Enchilada Sauce
1   teaspoon oregano
12 ounces canned corn, drained
8   ounces Chopped HATCH Green Chile
4   ounces chopped red bell pepper
1½ cups quick-cooking rice
1   cup grated Parmesan cheese
1   cup sliced black olives
1   bag of tortilla chips

Heat oil and garlic to medium hot and add lamb strips. Cook the lamb until it loses its pink color. Add the stock, enchilada sauce and oregano. Bring to a boil, reduce heat to a simmer and cover for 5 minutes. Add the corn, chiles and bell peppers. Bring to a full boil and stir in the rice. Cover and let stand according to the directions on the rice package or until all the moisture is absorbed. Fluff with fork. Serve with grated cheese, black olives, and tortilla chips.

Serves 4

Chapter Ten

Classy Casseroles and Breads

Green Chile Casserole

Early New Mexicans, having no easy way to commute between villages, would go to a wedding or Christmas fiesta and stay several days. They really knew how to party. You can use the following dish for such a party, too.

5	large tomatoes
4	whole eggs, lightly beaten
½	cup evaporated milk
1	teaspoon salt, or to taste
¼	teaspoon black pepper, or to taste
16	ounces HATCH green chiles, whole
8	ounces grated Jack cheese,
8	ounces grated longhorn cheese
¼	cup HATCH Nacho Jalapeños

Heat a small saucepan and scald each of the tomatoes for 30 to 45 seconds, to make them easy to peel. Peel the tomatoes and cut them in half. Remove the seeds, cut the tomatoes in ¼-inch slices and set them aside. Beat the eggs with the milk and add salt and pepper to taste. Set aside. Butter a 9" x 13" casserole and add a layer of chiles, then a layer of tomatoes, salt and pepper to taste, and a sprinkling of the cheeses to cover lightly. Do this until you use up all the chiles and tomatoes. Pour the egg mixture into the casserole and add the remaining cheese. Top with Jalapeños if you like it hot, and bake for 30 to 40 minutes at 350 degrees F.

Serves 5

Agua Fria Casserole

In old Santa Fe, there was no running water. Water from the Sangre de Cristo mountains ran down into town via the Santa Fe River. *Agua Fria* means cool water.

1   tablespoon corn oil
½   teaspoon celery salt
½   teaspoon garlic salt
1   pound pork shoulder, cut in ½-inch cubes
2   onions, chopped
1   can of tomato soup
1   can of water
4   ounces Chopped HATCH Green Chile
1   small jar roasted red peppers, chopped
¼   teaspoon paprika
     water
2   cups uncooked thin or medium egg noodles
¼   teaspoon black pepper
½   cup grated Longhorn cheese

Heat a Dutch oven with enough oil to brown the meat. While it is heating, mix the celery and garlic salts and rub them into the meat cubes. Brown the onions. Next add the meat and brown it. Now add the canned tomato soup and a can of water, the green and red peppers, and the paprika. Bring to a boil, lower to a simmer, cover and cook for 90 minutes. During the last 30 minutes, bring another pot of salted water to a boil, add the noodles and cook according to the directions on the package or until the noodles are *al dente*. Drain and rinse the noodles, and add them to the pot of simmering meat and vegetables 10 minutes before serving. Just before serving, add the black pepper and stir in the cheese to blend.

Serves 4

Chile and Cheese Stuffed French Bread

2   whole onions, chopped
8   ounces Chopped HATCH Green Chile
16   ounces grated Jack cheese
16   ounces sliced black olives
1   large loaf French bread

Mix the onions, chiles, cheese and olives. Slice the loaf lengthwise and remove the center from both sliced sides. Stuff both sides of the loaf and put the loaf back together. Put some stuffing on top and wrap in aluminum foil. Bake in a 300-degree oven for 20 to 25 minutes until the cheese melts. Slice and serve.

Serves 8

Blue Corn Green Chile Muffins

Blue corn, or Indian corn, is grown mostly in New Mexico and is a well-kept culinary secret. This nutty, earthy corn offers the perfect consistency and flavor for a green chile, walnut treat.

1½ cups fine-ground blue corn meal (available by mail order and from gourmet shops)
1   cup all-purpose flour
1   tablespoon salt
1   tablespoon baking powder
2   tablespoons sugar
1¾ sticks margarine, melted
¼   cup minced onions
1   clove garlic, minced
2   large eggs
1   cup low-fat milk
½   cup Chopped HATCH Green Chile
½   cup chopped walnuts
2   tablespoons fresh cilantro, chopped

Preheat the oven to 450 degrees. Combine the blue corn meal, flour, salt, baking powder, and sugar in a large bowl. In another bowl, whisk together the margarine, onion, and garlic. Add the eggs, milk, chile, walnuts, and cilantro, whisking continually.

Add the flour mixture in small amounts until the batter is completely combined. Pour the batter into 12 well-greased ¹/²-cup muffin tins. Bake the muffins for 18 to 20 minutes, or until they are golden. Turn them out onto racks and let them cool.

Makes 12 muffins.

There are two ways to spell the best food going: chile and chili. Chile is the official spelling in New Mexico for the food which, along with the pinto bean, make up the official state vegetables. Chile is considered to be the ingredient. Chili, on the other hand, is best-known in Texas and is a cooked dish—using chile as the principal spice of choice. Most chileheads really don't care how it's spelled as long as there is an adequate supply!

Slightly Spicy Cornbread

This recipe makes traditional corn bread or muffins, which is always good served with chile con carne.

1	cup flour
1	cup corn meal
2	tablespoons sugar
2½	teaspoons baking powder
1	cup skim milk
2	whole eggs, lightly beaten
1	teaspoon HATCH Red Enchilada Sauce
2	tablespoons vegetable oil
4	ounces Diced HATCH Green Chile
¼	cup chopped red bell peppers

In a bowl, mix the flour, cornmeal, sugar, and baking powder. In a measuring cup, combine milk, eggs, enchilada sauce and oil. Stir this mixture into the flour mixture just until moistened. Fold the chile and red pepper into batter. Set aside. Lightly butter an 8-inch cast iron skillet or a 12-cup muffin pan. Pour the batter into the skillet or fill the muffin cups ¾ full. Bake in a preheated 425-degree oven for 20 minutes for bread, or 15 minutes for muffins.

Serves 6

Robert's Cranberry Chile Cheese Bread

Chile Pepper Magazine Publisher Robert Spiegel contributed this excellent recipe. This bread is his favorite holiday baking tradition.

4   cups flour
1   cup sugar
1½   teaspoons baking powder
½   teaspoon soda
½   teaspoon salt
4   tablespoons Chopped HATCH Green Chile
½   cup crushed walnuts
1½   cups grated cheddar cheese
1   cup fresh cranberries, halved
1   egg, beaten
2   tablespoons margarine or shortening
1½   tablespoons grated orange peel
juice from 1 orange, mixed with enough water to yield ¾ cup liquid

Mix dry ingredients in a bowl, cut margarine into dry mixture. Combine wet ingredients in another bowl, then stir into the dry mixture. Pour into two greased loaf pans, bake at 350 for 60-70 minutes.

Yield: 2 loaves

Fiesta Cheese and Chile Bread

In 1851, historian Buckingham Smith, at the American Legation in Madrid, Spain, discovered the *Narrative of Alvar Núñez Cabeÿa de Vaca*. This dusty tome had lain for centuries before being re-introduced into the knowledge of the world. It revealed that Cabeÿa had been over the Santa Fe Trail fully five years before Coronado.

1	cup yellow cornmeal
1	cup flour
2	teaspoons sugar
1	teaspoon baking soda
1	teaspoon baking powder
1	teaspoon salt
¼	teaspoon garlic powder
1½	cups milk
1	cup minced onions
¼	cup HATCH Nacho Jalapeños
2	eggs, lightly beaten
1	cup grated Sharp Cheddar cheese

If you like, dice the chiles and then proceed with the recipe. If you like to bite on something hotter, leave the Jalapeños in rings.

Mix the dry ingredients in a mixing bowl. Allow the milk to come to room temperature and add it to the onions and chiles in another bowl. Take the room-temperature eggs and fold them into the grated cheese. Preheat the oven to 350 degrees. Combine all the liquid ingredients. Whisk the wet ingredient mixture into the dry a little at a time, incorporating well. Pour the batter into a buttered 9-inch cast iron skillet or casserole and bake for 40 to 50 minutes. Bread is done when a toothpick comes out cleanly.

Serves 8

Many of the families that farm the Hatch valley have been growing and selling chiles for generations.

Dave DeWitt

Quingombo Quemado

In the 1820s Governor Antonio Narbona built a sundial eight feet tall in the center of the Santa Fe Plaza. On it was the Latin inscription, VITA FUGIT SICUT UMBRA, meaning "life flees like a shadow." Governor Narbona loved okra, and you will too.

3	tablespoons rendered bacon fat or shortening
2½	cups fresh or frozen okra
2½	cups canned tomatoes
4	ounces Chopped HATCH Green Chile
2	white onions, chopped
1	tablespoon sugar
1	teaspoon paprika
½	teaspoon salt
1	pinch black pepper

Heat a large skillet or Dutch oven and add the fat or shortening. When the fat is nearly smoking, add the okra, tomatoes, green chiles and onions. Saute 5 minutes or until onions wilt a little. Add the sugar, paprika, salt and pepper. Add water if necessary. Cover and simmer nearly 60 minutes. The okra and tomato juices will form a sauce. This is most delicious as a vegetable dish to serve with ham.

Serves 8

Vibrant Vegetable Puff

For the pastry:
½   cup butter
1   cup water
⅛   teaspoon salt
⅛   teaspoon black pepper
1   cup flour
4   whole eggs
½   cup grated sharp Cheddar cheese

For the filling:
1   cup chopped onions
¼   cup butter
8   ounces fresh small mushrooms, sliced
½   teaspoon salt
1   tablespoon flour
½   cup hot water
3   medium tomatoes, sliced
4   ounces chopped HATCH green chile
½   cup grated Jack cheese

To make the puff dough

Melt the butter in the water and bring to a boil. Add the salt and pepper, then the flour, a spoonful at a time, and stir constantly until a ball forms. Cool slightly. Add the eggs, one at a time, beating hard with each addition. Blend in the cheese. Spoon the mixture into a well-greased, ten-inch pie pan or flat casserole. When done, set aside, covered to prevent drying out.

For the filling

Saute the onions in butter until golden. Add the mushrooms and heat through. Add the salt and sprinkle the flour on top. Add the hot water and boil until the flour, onion, and mushroom mixture thickens. Stir in the tomatoes and simmer for 2 minutes. Add the chile and cheese, and fold all together. Pour the mix into the center of the pastry, pushing the pastry up around the sides of the pan. Sprinkle with grated cheese and bake in a preheated 400-degree oven for 40 minutes.

Serves 4

A Marriage Made in Hatch

Chile Pepper magazine editor Dave DeWitt married his third wife, Janet, in 1983 at the police station in Hatch. The chief of police stood as witness.

Green Chile and Eggplant

This dish makes a great vegetarian taco filling.

1	eggplant
3	tablespoons olive oil
4	ounces Chopped HATCH Green Chile
2	onions, sliced
2	large tomatoes, sliced
½	teaspoon salt
2	teaspoons paprika

Peel and dice the eggplant into ½-inch pieces. Heat the olive oil in a saute pan large enough to hold all the ingredients. When the oil is almost smoking, add the chile and onions and saute until they soften. Next, add the eggplant and tomatoes. Season with salt and paprika to taste. Cover the pan and simmer 20 minutes.

Serves 4

Rice Stuffed Bell Peppers

4   green bell peppers, tops removed, deveined and seeded
4   tablespoons chopped onions
4   tablespoons chopped red bell pepper
4   tablespoons Chopped HATCH Green Chile
2   slices of bacon, fried and crumbled
3   cups tomatoes
3   cups cooked rice
    liquid hot sauce (optional)
    butter or margarine
4   tablespoons brown sugar
4   teaspoons lemon juice

Adjust the heat in these baked bell peppers by using milder or hotter green chiles, as your taste directs. Cut the top one-half to three-quarters of an inch off the bell peppers. Use the top parts with the chopped ingredients called for. Remove the veins and seeds. Set aside. Saute the chopped onions, chopped red bell pepper, and green chile in the bacon. Add the tomatoes and break them up with the back of a spoon. Add the cooked rice. If the filling isn't spicy enough, add some liquid hot sauce to taste. Fill the bell peppers, top with butter, and sprinkle on the brown sugar and lemon juice. Bake in a glass casserole to which a little warm water has been added to prevent scorching. Bake at 350 degrees for 30 minutes.

Serves 4

Chiles have been the subject of many fables. One of the oddest is that the Indians would take a bush of chiles wiped with tar or oil, ignite it, and throw it in the direction of their enemies. The smoke from the burning chiles was so pungent that it would make the eyes water and the throat cough, thereby distracting the combatants.

Calabacitas con Queso

With its combination of chiles, corn and squash, this simple yet flavorful dish is a wonderful celebration of the bounty of traditional New Mexico-grown crops.

2 tablespoons margarine
1 large onion, chopped
1 can corn, drained
4 ounces Diced HATCH Green Chile
2 zucchini squash, sliced
2 cups grated cheddar cheese

Preheat the oven to 350 degrees F. Melt the margarine in a skillet and sautee the onion. In a large bowl, stir together the corn, green chile, onion, zucchini and two-thirds of the cheese in a large bowl, then pour the mixture into a 3-quart glass casserole dish. Top with the remaining cheese and bake for 30 minutes. Serve with warm tortillas and butter as a meal, or serve as a side dish to an entree.

Serves 4

Stuffed Onions Monterey

Monterey is a name that appears all over the Americas. The Spanish, like the Germans, are fond of taking two or more words, chopping off a bit of one and adding the other to make a new word. *Monterey* is just such a word, consisting of two parts: *monte*, meaning mountain, and *rey*, meaning king. As Spanish puts the noun before the adjective, the meaning is: king's mountain.

4   large yellow or white onions
4   ounces ground turkey
4   ounces Diced HATCH Green Chile
4   ounces grated Jack cheese
2   ounces chopped black olives
½   cup bread crumbs

Preheat the oven to 350 degrees F. Parboil the onions 5 to 10 minutes. Remove the centers. Mix the turkey, diced green chile, Jack cheese, black olives and bread crumbs. Fill the openings with the mixture. Top the onions with a little cheese. Put the onions in a glass casserole and pour a little hot water into the casserole to prevent scorching. Bake for 30 minutes.

Serves 4

Corn and Green Chile

2   tablespoons butter or margarine
½   cup chopped scallions
⅔   cup Chopped HATCH Green Chile
1¼ cups canned tomatoes
½   teaspoon salt
2½ cups canned whole kernel corn
1½ cups grated Jack cheese

Heat the butter or margarine in a large skillet. Saute the scallions until translucent. Add the chile, tomatoes and salt. Cook until tender. Add the corn and simmer for five minutes. Remove from the heat and stir in the cheese until melted. Serve immediately.

Serves 6

Colache

This squash side dish makes use of fresh pumpkin. It is an unusual switch from zucchini, or beans and rice.

1   quart fresh pumpkin
1   tablespoon lard or shortening
8   ounces HATCH Picante sauce
1   pinch salt
4   tablespoons Chicken Stock Santa Fe or as needed (see page 63)

Open a pumpkin and remove the seeds. Slice away the skin and cube the pumpkin meat into large dice. Heat the lard in a large pot, add the diced pumpkin and saute five minutes. Add the picante sauce, salt and enough stock to prevent scorching. Lower the heat to just a simmer for 45 minutes.

Serves 8

Amusing characters like these decked-out green chile pods can be had at the Hatch Chile Festival, which occurs over Labor Day weekend each year.

Savory Spanish Rice

In 1829 Antonio Armijo extended the Old Spanish Trail from Santa Fe to San Diego in California. Following in Jedediah Smith's trail, Armijo also visited El Pueblo de Los Angeles, known then only as El Pueblo. Armijo traded Missouri mules to California and brought back olives and wine.

½   cup chopped onion
2   tablespoons corn oil
1   pound lean ground beef
¼   pound chorizo or Italian Sausage (see Colonel Hatch's Chorizo, page 102)
12 ounces spicy tomato juice
1   cup rice
4   ounces Chopped HATCH Green Chile
¼   teaspoon salt, or to taste
1   pinch black pepper
12 black olives, sliced
½   cup grated Jack or Cheddar cheese

Saute the onion in the oil until it turns translucent. Add the meats and saute until they lose their pink color. Drain the excess fat. Add the tomato juice, rice and green chile to the pan. Quickly bring to a boil, lower to a simmer and cover. Simmer until the rice is cooked (check for doneness after 20 minutes). Remove lid, add salt and pepper to taste, stir well. Just before serving, add the olives and sprinkle grated cheese over the top.

Serves 8

Manzano Potatoes*

2   whole cloves garlic, peeled
¼   cup olive oil
1   large baking potato, sliced
¼   pound chicken, shredded
½   teaspoon oregano
1½ tablespoons HATCH Picante Sauce
1   tablespoon minced green onions
½   cup grated Mozzarella cheese
⅛   cup sliced black olives, drained
⅛   cup sliced HATCH Nacho Jalapeños

Put the cloves of garlic in a jar and pour the olive oil over and set aside for one week. The olive oil will take on the flavor of the garlic without the sharp garlic taste. Wash and dry the potato and slice them into rounds ¼-inch thick. Arrange the slices on a heatproof platter in a single layer. Brush the slices, top and bottom, with the garlic oil. If more garlic flavor is desired, press a few cloves and dot the potatoes with them. Cover with plastic wrap. Microwave at full power for 4 to 5 minutes or until the potatoes are tender. If your microwave does not have a turntable, turn the dish once at 2 to 3 minutes. Combine the cooked chicken, oregano, picante sauce, and onions in a bowl. Stir well. Remove the potatoes from the microwave and spoon a teaspoon of mixture onto each potato round. Sprinkle with cheese and push an olive or jalapeño slice into the center of each piece. Cover and microwave at full power for 60 seconds or until the cheese is melted. Serve immediately.

Serves 3-4
*Please note this recipe requires advance preparation.

Cascara de Papas

The potato originated in the South American Andes, near the present-day country of Peru. It was not a very popular vegetable until the 18th century. In France, the potato was not considered worthy of eating until Augustin Parmentier convinced Louis XV that the potato was a worthwhile foodstuff. After the French adopted the potato, Parmentier had a holiday named in his honor.

8   large potatoes
     butter or margarine
12   ounces grated Jack cheese
½   cup HATCH Picante Sauce
½   cup chopped or sliced black olives
½   cup HATCH Nacho Jalapeños
½   cup sliced green onions
2   whole avocados

Wash and dry the potatoes. Rub the skins with butter. Bake the potatoes in a preheated 400-degree oven for 45 minutes. Remove, and immediately pierce the skin in several places with a fork. Rest 10 minutes or longer. Cut along the length and remove some of the potato meat. Save the removed potato for mashed potatoes or some other use. Mix the cheese, picante sauce, sliced or chopped olives, jalapeños and green onions well. Stuff the potato skins with the mix and reheat in a 450-degree oven for 5 to 10 minutes, no longer. Mash the avocados, mix with more picante sauce, and serve the skins with the guacamole in another bowl.

Makes 16 potato skins

Cerrillos Red Chile and Beans

2   bacon slices
1   clove garlic, minced
¼   cup chopped onions
1   cup chopped celery
½   pound lean ground beef
½   cup HATCH Red Enchilada Sauce
1   teaspoon salt, or to taste
¼   teaspoon pepper, or to taste
1   cup canned kidney beans, drained

In a Dutch oven, fry the bacon over low heat until almost crisp. Remove and wrap the bacon in a paper towel and set aside. Saute the garlic, onion and celery. Remove the vegetables and keep warm in a preheated oven. Brown the beef in the Dutch oven and when well cooked, add the enchilada sauce and salt and pepper to taste. Return the vegetables to the pot and stir well. Add the kidney beans. Raise the heat and bring to a simmer. Simmer about 60 minutes, stirring occasionally. Crumble or chop the bacon and sprinkle it over the bowls of chile. Serve with a side of your favorite salsa and warm flour tortillas.

Serves 4

Green Chile Frittata

This recipe is a blend of Italian and Southwestern cuisine. We guarantee any lover of traditional frittata will adore this Southwestern version.

1	tablespoon olive oil
8	ounces HATCH green chile, 4 ounces chopped, 4 ounces whole
¼	cup sliced mushrooms
1	cup sliced onions
8	eggs
½	cup Ricotta cheese
2	tablespoons lemon juice
½	teaspoon crushed oregano
¼	teaspoon salt
1	pinch pepper
	fresh oregano, for garnish
¼	cup grated Parmesan cheese

In a large non-stick skillet with oven-proof handle, heat the olive oil over medium heat. When the oil is hot, add the chopped green chile, mushrooms and onions and saute about 5 minutes until the onions are tender. Remove from the heat. Set aside 8 mushroom slices and tear 4 whole chiles into 8 strips. Add more oil, if necessary. Beat together the eggs, ricotta cheese, lemon juice, oregano, salt and pepper until blended. Pour this over the vegetables. Put the flame to low. Cover and cook until eggs are almost set, about 5 to 7 minutes. Remove the skillet from the heat and uncover. Arrange the green chile strips in spoke-like fashion over the eggs. Place the mushroom slices between the chile strips. Broil 6 inches from the heat until the eggs are set, about 3 to 5 minutes. Garnish with fresh oregano leaves. Cut into wedges, sprinkle with the Parmesan cheese and serve.

Serves 6

Pasta de la Frontera

The earliest settlers along the frontier brought this pasta dish. When the border moved south, this recipe stayed behind to feed the hungry traveler along the old Santa Fe Trail.

4   ounces Colonel Hatch's Chorizo (see page 102)
2   tablespoons butter or margarine
4   ounces angel hair pasta
1   small onion, diced
1   teaspoon salt
1   teaspoon red chile powder
1   cup tomatoes
2   cups water
1   cup grated Parmesan cheese

Heat a skillet and crumble and cook the chorizo. Drain it and keep it warm. Heat the butter in a large skillet. Brown the pasta. Mix in the remaining ingredients except the chorizo and cheese, adding just enough water to cover. Simmer 15 minutes, remove cover and cook until almost dry, about 5 minutes longer. Add the chorizo, sprinkle the Parmesan cheese over and serve.

Serves 2

Chile & Ricotta Rellenos

12 ounces Ricotta cheese
2   whole eggs, lightly beaten
1   tablespoon chervil
1   teaspoon sage
6   HATCH Whole Green Chiles
    oil for frying
2   eggs, lightly beaten, for dipping
1   cup flour

Mix the Ricotta cheese with 2 eggs and the chervil and sage. Stuff the herbed cheese into the chiles and close with toothpicks. Heat ½ inch of oil in a skillet. Dip the chiles in beaten egg, then dust in flour and fry golden brown. Remove the toothpicks and serve with beans and rice.

Serves 3

Pancho's Chile and Papas

When Francisco "Pancho" Villa sacked Columbus, New Mexico in 1916, he became the only soldier and expeditionary leader to ever dare to invade the United States of America. Columbus, New Mexico has a small park named in General Villa's honor.

2   whole large potatoes
2   quarts water
1   tablespoon salt
2   tablespoons olive oil
½   cup chopped onions
15   ounces HATCH Red Enchilada Sauce
1   clove garlic, minced
½   teaspoon oregano
½   teaspoon thyme
½   cup grated Jack cheese

Cook the potatoes in boiling, salted water. When done, remove and drain dry. Slice and set them aside, wiping a very thin layer of olive oil on both sides of each slice. In a glass casserole, put down a layer of potatoes, and over them, a layer of onions. Add a little garlic, oregano and thyme. Cover the first layer with enchilada sauce. Add the remaining potato slices and onions as the next layer. Pour a little more enchilada sauce over and sprinkle more spices. Sprinkle the cheese as the top layer. Bake in a 350-degree oven until thoroughly heated and the cheese starts to brown and bubble.

Serves 4

Governor's Palace Pasta

The Governor's Palace in Santa Fe, founded in 1609, is the oldest municipal building in the United States. For three hundred years thereafter, Spanish was the official language. Even after New Mexico was admitted as a state to the Union in 1912, the law books continued to be printed in Spanish.

2   tablespoons butter
4   ounces angel hair pasta or Mexican fideo
1   small onion, diced
2   ounces Chopped HATCH Green Chile
1   teaspoon salt
1   teaspoon red chile powder
1   cup chopped tomatoes
15 ounces Chicken Stock Santa Fe (see page 63)
1   cup grated Parmesan cheese

This is an authentic old-style recipe. If you can find Mexican *fideo* in skeins, by all means use it. If not, angel hair pasta will do. Heat the butter in a large skillet. Brown the pasta, moving it around constantly so it does not burn. Mix in the remaining ingredients, adding just enough chicken stock to cover the mixture. Cover the pot and simmer 15 minutes, then remove the cover and cook until almost dry, about 5 to 10 minutes longer.

Serves 2

Putting out the Fire

Even the most veteran chilehead can bite into an enchilada or relleno too hot to handle! One good way to cool down your mouth is to eat fruit in sweet syrup. Home-canned cling peaches are hard to beat, but other sweet items, such as jam and jelly, honey, milk, cold beer or non-diet pop seem to help close the pores in the mouth.

The first regular mail service was inaugurated between Independence, Missouri and Santa Fe on July 1st, 1850. The contract called for regular deliveries. Prior to that, mail service was available only when somebody decided to make the trip.

Desert Polenta

For the polenta:
3   cups water
1   teaspoon salt
¾   cup Italian polenta
1   pinch nutmeg

For the filling:
1   cup spaghetti sauce
4   ounces Chopped HATCH Green Chile
4   ounces boneless, cooked chicken breasts
½   cup grated Parmesan cheese

In a stainless steel pot, bring the water to a boil and add the salt. sprinkle the polenta into the boiling water a tablespoon at a time, stirring constantly. Add the nutmeg. When all the polenta has been added, lower the flame to a low boil and cook for 40 to 45 minutes, stirring frequently. Add the spaghetti sauce during the last 15 minutes the polenta is cooking. During the last 5 minutes, add the green chile and chicken. Pour into a serving bowl or individual plates, and sprinkle with the cheese.

Serves 4

The town of Hatch takes on a Fiesta air when it's Chile Festival time.

Eduardo Fuss

Spicy Yogurt Relish

Originally part of Hindu cuisine, this adaptation is a wonderful accompaniment to hot and spicy dishes of all sorts.

4	tablespoons wine vinegar
½	lemon, for juice only
1	clove garlic, minced
1	teaspoon Dijon mustard
1	teaspoon HATCH Nacho Jalapeños, minced
¼	teaspoon salt
½	cup unflavored yogurt
1	large cucumber, grated
1	small red onion, thinly sliced

Mix the vinegar, lemon juice, garlic, mustard, jalapeños, and salt. Stir in the yogurt and whisk all together to make a sauce. Toss with the cucumbers and onion. Chill and toss again before serving. Serve on a bed of rice, or with grilled chicken or beef.

Serves 6

Hellish Relishes and Chutneys

Padre's Old Fashioned Pear Relish

3   pounds hard-fleshed fresh pears (any winter variety)
4   ounces red bell pepper, roasted and marinated
4   ounces Chopped HATCH Green Chile
1   tablespoon HATCH Nacho Jalapeños
1½   onions
1½   cups vinegar
1½   cups sugar
½   teaspoon salt

Peel the pears and core them. Using the blade of a food processor, shred the pears, remove to a colander or sieve and drain almost dry. Save the juice to drink. Meanwhile, chop the red bell pepper, green chiles, jalapeños, and onions. Combine with all the remaining ingredients and the pears in a stock pot and bring to a boil for 20 minutes. Pack in canning jars and process in a boiling water bath for 10 minutes.

Makes 2 quarts of relish

Coronado Chile Relish

½   pound red bell peppers
½   pound gold bell peppers
1   pound eggplants
1   tablespoon HATCH Nacho Jalapeños
1   28-ounce can Chopped HATCH Green Chile
2   cloves garlic, crushed
1   teaspoon salt
9   tablespoons olive oil
4   tablespoons wine vinegar

To roast and marinate the bell peppers:
Char the bell peppers on a grill or griddle about 20 minutes, turning frequently to prevent scorching. Place the peppers in a one-gallon plastic zip-lock bag. Set aside 20 minutes. Remove from the bag, skin, devein, de-stem and roughly tear them up. Put in a jar with a mixture of half water, half wine vinegar and refrigerate overnight.

To make the relish:
Skin the eggplant and dice it. Mince the jalapeño. Put them in a stainless steel pot. Add the green chile and the bell peppers, garlic, salt, oil and vinegar. Cook until smooth, like a fine chutney, about 30 minutes. Serve hot as a spread for warm flour tortillas.

For a milder version double the garlic, omit the jalapeño, and use lemon juice instead of vinegar. Serve this version cold.

Makes 1½ quarts of relish

The Keeper of Records

June Rutherford is a very careful record keeper. Her detailed journals are a virtual history of the development of the chile industry in the Hatch Valley. Her greatest pride is in the many calls from growers telling her how great their crop was and thanking her for providing the highest-quality seed.

Hatch Hot Relish

8   green tomatoes
26 ounces Chopped HATCH Green Chile
1   head cabbage
¼   cup salt
1½ cups cider vinegar
1   cup sugar
½   cup mustard seeds
1   tablespoon celery seeds
1   tablespoon dry mustard
5   ounces red chile powder
1   tablespoon ground cumin
1   teaspoon crushed oregano
3 to 4   cloves garlic, mashed
1   teaspoon salt

Have all the ingredients ready. Chop the tomatoes in a food processor. Mix them in a large bowl with the chiles. Remove the tough outer leaves of the cabbage and discard them. Chop or shred the cabbage. In a crock or food-grade plastic bucket, put a layer of cabbage, then the chile and tomato mix. Sprinkle a portion of the salt over the first layer. Repeat this layering and salting until all are used up, making the last layer of salt. Allow the crock to rest for 24 hours, covered. The next day, drain the excess liquid. Do this draining in batches in a colander. Heat the vinegar in a covered soup kettle large enough to hold the vegetables. When the vinegar is at a simmer, add the drained vegetables. Next, add the sugar and mustard and celery seeds. Stir to mix thoroughly. Return to a simmer on low heat. Turn off the heat and add the dry mustard, stirring to prevent lumping, and then the chile powder, cumin, oregano, garlic and salt. Pack into hot jars and top with more cider vinegar if necessary.

Makes 2 quarts

Green Chile Chutney

Raisins, although no longer commonly produced in New Mexico, were an important crop during the 19th century for the local market.

3½ cups cider vinegar
5   ounces Chopped HATCH Hot Green Chile
5   ounces HATCH Nacho Jalapeños, optional
24   large, ripe tomatoes, quartered
4   large onions, chopped
½   pound seedless raisins
2   cups sugar
2   ounces fresh ginger root, peeled and chopped
4   tablespoons salt
1   stick cinnamon
6   whole cloves

You must use hot canned chiles for this recipe. Use the extra jalapeños only if you like chutney very hot. In a large stockpot, add the vinegar, chiles, quartered tomatoes, chopped onions, raisins, sugar, ginger, salt and spices. Bring to a low boil for 3½ hours. Bottle in sterilized jars.

Makes 2 quarts

Spicy Chile Butter

This spicy butter can be rubbed on steaks or chops before cooking them. It can be spread on them after cooking as well. Use this fine flavor on vegetables, popcorn, breads or toast.

1   stick butter
1   clove garlic
½   teaspoon lemon juice
½   teaspoon HATCH Nacho Jalapeño juice
1   tablespoon diced marinated red bell peppers

Let the butter come to room temperature. Mash the garlic with the lemon juice and jalapeño juice. Next, add the diced bell peppers. Stir to mix. Refrigerate for up to two weeks, or freeze for up to one month.

Serves 8

The dam at Elephant Butte Lake is largely responsible for the existence of the verdant chile fields of the Hatch valley.

Dave Jackson

Bizcochitos

These traditional sugar cookies were made with lard a century ago, as the New Mexicans never cooked with butter. Use butter or lard as you prefer.

1   cup lard or butter
¾   cup sugar, ¼ cup reserved for topping
1   egg
1   tablespoon anise seeds
3   cups flour
1½   teaspoons baking powder
½   teaspoon salt
3   tablespoons brandy or rum
2   teaspoons cinnamon

Preheat the oven to 350 degrees. Put the lard in a mixer bowl and beat it creamy. Sprinkle in the sugar and beat until dissolved. Beat in the egg. Crush the anise seeds in a mortar or on a work surface with the flat of a knife. In another bowl, mix the seeds, flour, baking powder, and salt, then sprinkle into the bowl with the fat and mix. Add the brandy or rum at the end. Remove the dough and roll out to cookie thickness, less than ¼-inch. Using a cookie cutter, make cut-outs. Ball up the scrap and roll out again, placing the cookies on ungreased baking sheets as you make them. Mix the reserved sugar and cinnamon and sprinkle it over the cookies. Bake in the oven 8 to 12 minutes or until golden brown. Cool on racks.

Makes 2-3 dozen cookies.

Chapter Fourteen

Diabolic Desserts

Tequila and Lime Cheesecake

This dessert is more likely to wake you up than put you to sleep. Over a century ago, tequila was sometimes referred to as *tanglefoot*. It was rumored that it could stagger a man at 300 feet from the bottle. Purchase enough limes to make fresh juice for this tangy dessert. Make the crust ahead of time and it will be easier to serve.

For the crust:
1½ cups unsalted pretzels
2   tablespoons sugar
1   stick margarine or butter

For the filling:
1   cup lemon-flavored yogurt
1   cup sugar
¼   cup margarine or butter
2   teaspoons lime zest
½   cup lime juice (reserve 2 tablespoons)
½   cup sweetened condensed milk
3   tablespoons cornstarch
¼   cup tequila
1   tablespoon orange-flavored cordial
1   cup whipping cream
2   tablespoons powdered sugar
2   limes
1   teaspoon kosher salt

In a food processor, crush the pretzels to a powder. Add the sugar while the blade is turning and throw in the margarine, 1 tablespoon at a time. When well blended (about 2 minutes), use the crust to line a lightly buttered 9-inch pie plate or springform pan. Set in the refrigerator, covered, to chill. Put the yogurt in a sieve and put the sieve in a deep bowl. Let the yogurt drain. When ready, return the yogurt to its carton or a bowl. Refrigerate.

In a double boiler, put the sugar, margarine, lime zest, lime juice less 2 tablespoons, and the condensed milk. Put the double boiler over a medium-high heat and stir for about 8 to 10 minutes. Mix the reserved lime juice with the cornstarch and add it to the double boiler. Stir to mix. Cook several minutes longer to thicken. Remove from the heat and add the tequila and orange-flavored liqueur. Stir to blend. Put the bowl in the refrigerator and chill for 45 to 60 minutes. Remove from the refrigerator and fold in the drained yogurt. Whip the cream and fold it into the mixture. Pour the mixture into the pie or cheesecake pan and smooth the top with a spatula. To garnish: slice the limes very thinly and dip them in the coarse salt. Decorate the top rim of the cheesecake with the limes. Chill 4 hours before serving and remove from the refrigerator 20 minutes before serving.

Santa Fe Hot Pecans

1   pound shelled pecans
⅓   cup butter
1   tablespoon Worcestershire sauce
½   teaspoon HATCH Hot Enchilada Sauce
¼   teaspoon pepper
1   teaspoon salt

Preheat the oven to 300 degrees. Place the nuts in a shallow baking pan. Combine all other ingredients, pour them over the nuts and stir well. Bake for 20 minutes, stirring twice during baking. Cool on paper towels. Store in airtight containers.

Hatch Hot Pecan Brittle

If you don't have pecans on hand, use peanuts. They are just as good.

2   cups sugar
1   cup Karo light corn syrup
¾   cup HATCH Red Enchilada Sauce
2   cups pecans
2   tablespoons butter
1   pinch salt

Lightly butter a baking sheet. In a heavy saucepan, mix the sugar, corn syrup, and the enchilada sauce. Stir over low heat until the sugar has completely dissolved. Then increase the heat to medium and cook, without stirring, until the syrup browns. Remove from the heat, and add the nuts and butter. Stir until the nuts are well-coated. Pour onto the buttered baking sheet, spreading the mixture quickly with a buttered spatula. Lightly sprinkle with the salt. It should be about ½-inch thick. Cool, break into pieces, and it's ready.

Fiery Fruit Cobbler

For the biscuits:
2 cups flour
3 teaspoons baking powder
½ teaspoon salt
½ cup shortening
1 cup milk

For the cobbler:
2 tablespoons water
½ cup sugar, or to taste
1 lemon, for both the juice and zest
3 pints fresh peaches
4 ounces Diced HATCH Green Chile
1 cup sweetened condensed milk

Preheat oven to 450 degrees. Mix the flour, baking powder and salt and sift one time. Cut in the shortening and mix until the dough forms crumbs. Mix in the milk to form a ball that doesn't stick to the sides of the bowl. On a floured board, knead the dough until it is not sticky to the touch, about 2 minutes. Roll out the dough to about ½-inch thick and cut into 2-inch rounds using a floured cutter.

Mix the water, sugar, zest and juice and set aside to make a syrup. sprinkle the peaches and chiles with the syrup and stir to coat. Place them in the bottom of a 9"x 12" glass baking dish and set the rounds on the fruit. Brush the dough with the sweetened condensed milk and dust with sugar. Bake until biscuits are golden brown, 30 to 40 minutes. Serve hot, straight from the oven, or at room temperature. Serve with ice cream or drizzled with sweetened condensed milk.

Serves 6

Day O' The Dead Empanadas

For the Dough:
2 cups flour
1 teaspoon salt
⅔ cup shortening
6 tablespoons ice water

For the Filling:
1 whole orange and zest
2 tablespoons butter
1 cup brown sugar
1 cup pumpkin puree, not presweetened
1 teaspoon cinnamon
   a pinch of ground cloves
1 whole egg
1 teaspoon water
½ cup sugar
1 teaspoon ground cinnamon

To make the empanada dough:

Mix the flour and salt together well. Add the shortening, using a fork or a pastry blender. Cut the shortening in as quickly as possible; that is, don't overmix. Add the ice water and mix until a crumbly dough is made. Put the dough in the refrigerator for 30 minutes before using it. Remove when ready, and roll it out to ½ inch thick

To make the filling:

Zest the orange and set it aside. Heat the butter in a pot and add the brown sugar. Stir until moistened. Add the pumpkin, cinnamon, clove, egg, and water. Taste the mixture and adjust the seasonings. The pumpkin puree should dry out during the 3 to 5 minutes of heating. Add the orange zest. Allow to cool, then refrigerate. The puree should be refrigerator temperature before attempting to make the empanadas. Mix the sugar and cinnamon and blend well. Set aside.

To fill the empanadas:

Using a coffee cup, cut out rounds. Fill each with a little of the filling. Fold the empanada in half, moistening the edge with a wet finger. Seal and impress the edge with the tines of a fork for a decorative edge. Bake in a preheated 400-degree oven for 15 minutes or until golden. Remove and sprinkle with the prepared sugar. Serve slightly warm, not cold.

Makes 24 empanadas

Bananas Borrachos.

3 tablespoons butter
4 tablespoons brown sugar
1 teaspoon vanilla
4 bananas, peeled
¼ cup Absolut Vodka
16 anisette cookies
1 can sweetened condensed milk
   whipped cream as needed

Melt the butter in a skillet. Add the brown sugar and vanilla and stir until melted. Next, add the bananas and saute until the mixture carmelizes on the sides of the bananas. Remove from the heat and pour the vodka over the bananas. Ignite the liquor and allow it to burn out, then put the pan aside.

On four plates, arrange four cookies on each, broken into fourths. Slice each banana into 6-8 pieces and arrange evenly on the plates over the cookies. Pour some sweetened condensed milk over the bananas and finish with a dollop of whipped cream.

Serves 4

Fiesta Cream Puffs

Taos native Kit Carson relates the tale of a greenhorn who, as part of a hunting party, went out from camp to shoot a buffalo. The greenhorn wandered about six hundred yards from camp and took aim at a buffalo grazing in a herd of six to ten. Several moments later, the hunter came running back through camp with the bull buffalo hot on his trail. The hunter and animal knocked over several tables, the day's food and a tent or two before Carson was able to get to his rifle. All in the party had a good laugh on the greenhorn, and from thereon he stuck around the camp, doing the cooking and other camp chores.

Puffs:

1	stick butter
1	cup boiling water
1	cup all-purpose flour
4	eggs

Filling:

1	11 ounces cream cheese, softened
½	cup powdered sugar
½	stick butter, softened
½	cup Hot Fudge Sauce
1	tablespoon red chile powder (Mexican if available)
½	teaspoon ground cinnamon

Topping:

½	cup hot fudge sauce
2	tablespoons sour cream
¼	teaspoon almond extract
¼	cup finely chopped roasted almonds

In a saucepan melt the butter in the boiling water. Add the flour all at once. Cook, stirring, til the mixture forms a ball. Remove from the heat. Cool slightly then add the eggs, one at a time, beating after each addition til the mixture is smooth. Drop by heaping tablespoonfuls onto a greased baking sheet. Bake at 450 degrees 10 minutes then lower the heat to 325 degrees and bake 25 minutes. Remove from the oven and split the puffs. Turn off the oven and put the puffs back in to dry, about 20 minutes, then cool. For the filling, beat together all ingredients until smooth. Fill each bottom puff half with the filling. Top with the other half. For the topping gently heat the sauce and sour cream in a pan, stirring. Add the extract; drizzle the topping over each puff and garnish with the nuts.

Makes 10

Red Chile Chocolate Mousse

Chocolate and red chile offer the perfect blending of heat and heaven.

2   **cups sour cream**
½   **cup sugar**
½   **cup crumbled macaroons**
3   **ounces unsweetened chocolate, melted**
1   **tablespoon rum or brandy**
1   **tablespoon red chile powder**
1   **teaspoon vanilla (Mexican, if available)**

Mix all ingredients together thoroughly. Spoon into a freezer tray and freeze for about 3 hours or until firm, but not rock-hard Scoop into glasses and sprinkle with shaved sweet chocolate.

Serves 4

Fantastic Flan

This dessert is a wonderful cool down for any fiery fare. Your guests will love the sweet, rich taste of this Mexican custard.

½   cup sugar
8   egg yolks
2   egg whites
1   14-ounce can sweetened condensed milk
1   13-ounce can evaporated milk
2   cups whole milk or water
1   teaspoon vanilla (Mexican, if available)

In a heavy skillet, melt the sugar, stirring constantly. When it is light brown, pour it into a 2-quart mold. Holding the mold with tongs, tip it quickly in all directions so that caramel coats the inside. Set the mold aside. Beat the eggs until thick. Beat in the condensed milk, evaporated milk, whole milk (or water), and vanilla. Pour the mixture into the prepared mold. Cover securely with a tight lid or with 3 layers of foil tied down. Place the mold on a rack in a pressure cooker with 2-3 cups of water (follow manufacturer's direction) and cook for 20 minutes after the pressure comes up. (It will take a bit longer at higher altitudes). Allow to cool rapidly. After the custard is chilled, turn it out onto a serving dish.

Serves   12

The Most Fabulous Frozen Margarita

OK, so maybe this isn't a traditional dessert. However, this icy concoction does go down smoothly before, during, or after any main meal in this book!

1½   cups tequila
8   fresh limes, or enough to make ½ cup juice
¼   cup Cointreau or Triple Sec
     crushed ice
     Kosher rock salt

Take 4 large goblets and rub the outer edges with a piece of lime section. Dip the goblet rims into the salt and then place the goblets into the freezer for at least 30 minutes.

Juice the limes and then place the lime juice, tequila, and Triple Sec in a blender. Add the crushed ice until the blender is half-full and then process. Taste the result and adjust the flavor by adding more Triple Sec to make it sweeter, more lime juice to make it tart. Pour into the frosted goblets and garnish each each with a slice of lime.

Serves: 4

Creamy Southwestern Blintzes

This German dessert is transformed into a Southwestern delight with the addition of HATCH green chile and piñons.

24 crepes (from the frozen food section of the grocery store)
½ cup cottage cheese
1 large pack (13 ounce) cream cheese
1 egg
1 teaspoon vanilla (Mexican, if available)
¼ teaspoon cinnamon
9 ounces Chopped HATCH Green Chile
¼ cup chopped seedless raisins
¼ cup piñons, minced
3 tablespoons butter or margarine
   cherry or plum jam
   sour cream

Prepare the crepes as directed, cooking on one side only. Stack waxed paper between crepes. Put cottage cheese in blender or food processor and blend smooth, or push through a sieve. Blend in the cream cheese, egg, vanilla, and cinnamon. Mix in raisins, chile, and piñons. Spoon a tablespoonful or two in the center of cooked side of each crepe. Fold the crepes up into little packages. Saute the packages in some of the butter in a large skillet. Cook until golden brown on each side, about 4 minutes, adding more butter as needed. Serve warm with sour cream and jam or confectioner's sugar.

Yield: 12 to 24, depending on the amount of filling used in each.

Simple Sopaipillas

Traditionally served with a pot of mesquite honey, sopaipillas are without doubt one of New Mexico's finest contributions to the culinary arts. While somewhat similar to the New Orleans beignet, they are usually larger in size.

¼   cup water
1½ cups milk
2   tablespoons sugar
1   package yeast
1   teaspoon salt
3   tablespoons lard or shortening at room temperature
1   cup unbleached whole wheat flour
4   cups all-purpose flour
    corn oil

For the dough:
Mix the water, milk, and sugar in a saucepan and heat the mixture until it reaches 155 degrees. If you have a microwave with a temperature probe, put the mixture into a measuring cup and heat it in your microwave to the proper temperature. When the chime sounds, sprinkle the yeast over and stir to mix. Set aside 5 minutes. Stir in the salt and lard. Put the flours in a mixer bowl. Attach the dough hook if you have one. Start the mixer and pour the shortened liquid into the bowl. If necessary, stop the mixer and use a spatula to push the dough back down. Restart and continue to add the liquid in a thin stream. Run the mixer 10 minutes. The dough-sponge should have pulled away from the sides of the mixer bowl. Flour a board. Remove the dough to the board and knead until the sponge is stiff. Return to the mixer bowl, cover with plastic wrap and allow to rise, in a warm place, for 60 minutes; then punch the dough down. You may now refrigerate the dough overnight, or roll it out for ready use.

For the sopaipillas:
Divide the room-temperature dough into 18 to 24 equal pieces. Using a rolling or tortilla pin,

roll the pieces out to a thickness of ⅛-inch and form into a somewhat square shape. In an electric frying pan with a temperature gauge, put about 2 inches of corn oil and heat to 350 degrees. If you don't have an electric utensil, heat a cast iron skillet or wok over a flame about ⅝ of an inch high. Allow the oil to heat up for 20 minutes before use. Using tongs, put the sopaipillas into the hot oil 2 or 3 at a time. Fry the first side until the dough puffs up. Turn and fry the other side, basting with a long-handled kitchen spoon. Don't fry longer than 2 minutes! Drain on brown paper on a baking sheet.

Makes 12 sopaipillas

HATCH Product List

The recipes in this book call for HATCH products. Most or all of these products are available nationally in large grocery store chains. Here is a listing of all the HATCH products called for in this book:

HATCH Whole Green Chiles

Chopped HATCH Green Chiles

Chopped HATCH Hot Green Chiles

Diced HATCH Green Chiles

HATCH Nacho Jalapeños

HATCH Red Enchilada Sauce

HATCH Hot Red Enchilada Sauce

HATCH Green Enchilada Sauce

HATCH Picante Sauce

HATCH Refried Beans

HATCH Refried Black Beans

HATCH Refried Beans With Green Chile

HATCH Taco Shells

HATCH Blue Corn Taco Shells

HATCH T.M.

Select

REFRIED BEANS

CHOLESTEROL FREE

NET WT 16 OZ (454 g)

The bright yellow background and distinctive HATCH red letters make HATCH brand products easy to identify in the grocery store.

Here is a partial list of mail order sources if HATCH products are not locally available:

Old Southwest Trading Company
P.O. Box 7545
Albuquerque, New Mexico 87196
1-800-748-2861

The New Mexico Connection
2833 Rhode Island, NE.
Albuquerque, New Mexico 87110
1-800-933-2736

Index

Be sure to look for these other wonderful Border Books titles:

Spice It Up!
The Art of Making Condiments
by Jeffree Itrich
ISBN 0-9623865-6-1
$12.95

California Mission Cookery
The Origins of California Cooking Revealed
by Mark Preston
ISBN 0-9623865-5-3
$15.95

A Taste of Ranching
Cooks and Cowboys
by Tom Bryant and Joel Bernstein
ISBN 0-9623865-7-X
$15.95

The West Indies Cookbook
Classic Recipes from the Spicy Caribbean
by Connie and Arnold Krochmal
ISBN 0-9623865-3-7
$9.95

The Blue Corn Cookbook
Unique and Traditional Recipes Featuring Blue Corn Cookery
by Celine-Marie Pascale
ISBN 0-9623865-1-0
$7.95

Fiery Appetizers
Seventy Hot and Spicy Hors d'Oeuvres
by Dave DeWitt and Nancy Gerlach
ISBN 0-9623865-2-9
$8.95

Coyote Cooks:
The Southwest Cookbook for Kids
by Carol Skrepcinski
ISBN 1-884374-07-7
$10.95

Jungle Feasts
An Adventurer's Cookbook
by Richard Sterling
ISBN 1-884374-00-X
$15.95

Continued on next page

The Edward S. Curtis Postcard Book
Vintage Photographs of Southwest Images
Edited by Dave DeWitt and Andrew Smith
ISBN 1-884374-04-2
$8.95

We also publish an assortment of beautiful calendars, and are always adding new titles to our inventory. For a complete catalog of our products, contact:

Border Books Publishers
P.O. Box 80780
Albuquerque, New Mexico 87198
(505) 254-0325